THE
LAST
SPARTANS

by Larry Ferazani

QUINLAN PRESS, INC. BOSTON

Published by Quinlan Press, Inc.
131 Beverly Street
Boston, MA 02114

Library of Congress
Catalog Card Number 85-71764
ISBN 0-933341-09-1

Printed in the United States of America
November, 1985

Translation of "The Spartan Monument" by H. Macnaghten.

To my sons, Larry and Stephen.

. . . let me speak to the yet unknowing world
How these things came about: so shall you hear
  Of carnal, bloody, and unnatural acts,
  Of accidental judgements, casual slaughters,
Of deaths put on by cunning and forced cause,
  And, in this upshot, purposes mistook
  Fall'n on the inventor's heads. . . .
But let this same be presently perform'd,
Even while men's minds are wild; lest more mischance,
On plots and errors, happen.

William Shakespeare, *Hamlet*

ACKNOWLEDGEMENT

To Sandra Bielawa, my editor, for her patience.

The events described in this book actually took place. Names, dates and locations have been changed to protect the privacy of real persons.

THE SPARTAN MONUMENT

Into the dark death cloud they passed, to set
Fame on their own dear land for fadeless wreath,
And dying died not. Valour lifts them yet
Into the splendour from the night beneath.

Simonides

••••*FORWARD*••••••••••

I have been a firefighter in Cambridge, Massachusetts, for seemingly a lifetime. To some, this city is the intellectual and cultural center of the universe, home to Harvard University and the Massachusetts Institute of Technology—two of the most prestigious schools in the country. To me, this city represents a never-ending pageantry of wealth and poverty. I grew up in this city, right outside the gates of Harvard University. I lived in a neighborhood called Kerry Corner, an Irish, working-class area of the city. Harvard University, in its appetite for real estate, was later to consume my neighborhood.

Growing up and working in Cambridge, I had an opportunity to be exposed to the affluence and influence of power. For example, every June the Rescue Company had the opportunity to work at Harvard's commencement; we were hired to assist in any medical emergency that might arise during the ceremonies. When the day-time festivities continued into the night, and while the graduates, guests and alumni partied, the big wrought-iron gates would close up on us, and we would return to the firehouse outside Harvard Yard, in a single moment leaving the smiling, sparkling eyes of the privileged to look into the sunken and searching eyes of the disadvantaged. We would leave this land of enchantment often to crawl moments later through a smoke-filled, dilapidated tenement house in search of nameless people, or to kneel on a urine-stained stairway next to a blood-soaked child caught in the middle of an ill-timed drug deal.

For ten years I responded from that firehouse outside Harvard Yard. I watched, and many times participated in, the frequently angry and chaotic events that this college city was involved in: from the Civil Rights movement and anti-war marches, to campus protests and the cause and effect they had on our lives. I participated in events that saw friends badly injured, some crippled and some killed.

Because of these events, seven years ago I sat down and wrote about the experiences I had while on the Cambridge Rescue Squad. It was a therapeutic exercise, an effort to purge myself of the emotional trauma that I encountered on a daily basis on the Rescue, which was impossible to discuss with friends, colleagues or even family. I wrote about the social degradation that unfolded in front of my eyes more rapidly than I was able to comprehend. At times I felt trapped in a five-by-ten-foot motorized capsule that carried victim after victim through the dimly lit and lonely streets. Sometimes I compressed chests or pumped air into lungs, sometimes I tried to control the pulsating arteries and spurting blood, and often I merely tried to relieve the effects of a repressive injury to the mind. It seemed as if the Rescue Squad was forsaken by mankind in that endless three-minute ride to the hospital.

This feeling of isolation as we sped down the lonely street made me realize that I would have to try to report these incidents to an imperceptive community.

···ONE···

The sound of the bells in the firehouse jolted the men on the
second floor out of bed. The bells signaled an alarm of fire on
Cambridge Street near Inman Square. Some men were still
fumbling with their clothes as others made it to the brass pole
taking them to the first floor of the building.

One of the firemen on the watch floor had brought the horses to
the quick-hitch suspended from the ceiling in front of the steam
engine. The horses were well-behaved and knew their positions.
Another fireman, down from upstairs, now joined the first and
helped him place the quick-hitch harness over the horses. Half-
dressed, a fireman slid down the pole; when he hit the large
wooden boards of the firehouse floor, he bolted toward the
kerosene lanterns hanging on either side of the steam engine,
lighting both and then returning them to their places.

"Get the door open!" a voice shouted. The big hinged door to
the firehouse was pushed out and over the cobblestone street. The
driver clutched the heavy leather straps in both hands like a
jockey waiting for the gate to open, holding steady on the reins.

The officer jumped up to the passenger seat, a narrow bench.
When in position, he looked around to see that everyone was

securely aboard. The steam engine now lighted and black smoke billowing from its chimney, he yelled an ''OK'' to the driver.

The driver, his large hands grasping the straps, signaled the horses, and they bolted forward onto the street. Down Cambridge Street the horses raced, their iron-clad hooves beating a steady rhythm and sending out sparks as they hit the cobblestones. The glow of the lanterns on the side of the engine and the enveloping smoke gave the big white horses a ghostly look, further reinforced by the eerie clanging of the fire bells echoing through the deserted night streets.

The officer could see the outline of a crowd of spectators in the street illuminated by the fire. The driver would have to be careful, he thought. He didn't want the horses trampling any of the people. The stable was fully involved in fire; fortunately, no buildings were next to it. The driver pulled back on the reins, slowing the horses to a walk. He would have to maneuver them toward the only hydrant on the street.

The officer jumped from his position on the engine to the ground. Off in the distance, he heard the bells of the oncoming ladder company. The fire was moving quickly: the stable was entirely engulfed in flames, and they could hear the whinnying of horses still trapped inside. It was an eerie, depressing sound. Hoses now charged with water, the firefighters moved toward the stable.

Suddenly there was a loud roar, and the building collapsed, sparks and flames leaping a hundred feet into the night sky. People were running and screaming; horses in the street bolted and reared up. Policemen tried to control the crowd while firemen tried to calm the horses.

Moving toward the collapsed stable, firemen now directed the stream of water onto the pile of burning rubble. All through the night, they washed down pockets of fire, shifting the rubble by hand to get at the deeply seated fire. By early morning, they were *exhausted from the night's battle. The fire now out, the men slowly mounted the steam engine. The driver slightly nudged the reins and the horses started their solemn parade back to the firehouse. The bowed heads and soot-stained faces of the men riding the cooled-down engine gave no hint of glory. The driver was particularly saddened: that week, his horses were to be replaced by a motorized piece of equipment. This final parade was marching into history. Only in the nostalgic reveries of their witnesses would these events live on.*

"They lost six horses in that fire," Jimmy Doherty said softly. We must have heard that story a hundred times over the years, and every time we heard it, there was another little twist to it. We all liked to hear about the old days in the firehouse, and Jimmy, a fire buff, could tell a story as good as anyone we knew.

Like the horses, the fire buffs I had known were becoming obsolete. When I first went on the Department, there were four or five buffs to every station. They came from all walks of life, and their hobby was to ride the apparatus, many times even helping us at a fire. Now, with liability and other rules, it had become increasingly more difficult for people like Jimmy to enjoy their hobby.

I always liked it when Jimmy came in. He would talk about the old days, how the Fire Department was, and tell stories of the firemen. He didn't stay long tonight, however. Finishing his coffee, he said, "I guess I'll run along. You guys are on again tomorrow night, aren't you?"

"Yeah, one more night," I answered.

"Well, I may drop in again tomorrow."

"OK, Jimmy. I hope we see you." I sat back in my chair, thinking about his story.

The sound of the fire phone broke the silence. Bobby Rinaldi, at the patrol desk, picked up the phone. He wrote down the information, at the same time pointing toward the apparatus, which meant we were going out. Bobby hung up the phone and repeated the message he had received from the fire alarm operator over the house speaker system, a report of smoke in the building at 233 Rindge Avenue. Charlie Williams was sliding the pole from the second floor; Dave Clark was running from the kitchen on the first floor as I reached the pump. I pulled my rubber coat from the front seat, at the same time kicking off my shoes and stepping into my boots, which were placed next to the pump. The overhead doors were going up as I jumped up into the passenger seat.

Both pieces of apparatus left the station at the same time, rolling out onto Massachusetts Avenue, a street that seemed to be congested with traffic twenty-four hours a day. Tonight wasn't any different. As we made our way up the street, we pulled right behind a line of traffic. Most of the cars pulled over to let us pass, but, as usual, one car stayed right in front of us. I hit the air horn to signal to the driver, but he continued to ignore sirens, lights, and horn. I kept hitting it, and finally the car pulled over just enough to let us pass. As we drove by, the driver looked up; he glared at us as if to say, "What did you want me to do?"

As we made our way through Sheridan Square, I could see the fire ahead of us, coming out of the window at around the twelfth floor of the twenty-two-story high-rise apartment building. I looked over at Jerry O'Brien. "We got troubles," I said, as I picked up the mike. We had only one engine company and one ladder company coming to this alarm. I radioed fire alarm to strike a box, which meant we would get an additional ladder truck, another two engine companies and the Rescue Company to respond to this location.

We pulled into the long driveway of the complex, and I told Jerry to hook up to the Fire Department standpipe connection in front of the building, which would allow us to bring water into the building. I jumped out of the pump and walked to the side of the wagon that had pulled in behind us. Charlie and Dave were already strapping on their Scott air packs; I grabbed my Scott and did the same. Looking up, I could see flames flaring against the dark sky.

Dave walked to the back of the wagon and unhooked the high-rise kit from its anchor on the back step. This consisted of a wooden box placed on a makeshift dolly the crew had put together to carry three fifty-foot lengths of one-and-a-half-inch hose and various tools and adapters for the standpipe connections. Unfortunately, vandals had destroyed the existing hoses in the building and stolen the adapters off the standpipe on every floor. Because of this, we had to bring an entire plumbing system with us.

We wheeled the kit through the front door into the lobby and over to the elevator bays. The Fire Department control panel had been pulled from the wall, which meant we could not control the elevators and had to wait for the car to come to the first floor after it had stopped at every floor on its way down. As we waited, I looked around to see if any tenants were leaving the building, but the lobby was empty. In most cases, tenants would either be running out of the building or shouting out the windows, but not at 233 Rindge

Avenue. The Fire Department was here at least twice a day, mostly on account of smoke from the incinerator chutes in the hallway.

The elevator finally made it to the first floor; we wheeled the kit on and climbed aboard. Just then, a tenant came running up to the elevator and stepped in.

"Hey," I said, "we've got a fire on the twelfth floor and you can't use the elevator."

He mumbled something I couldn't make out and stepped out of the elevator. As the door closed in his face, he turned and shouted, "You assholes!"

I pressed floor number eleven on the panel, the floor below the fire. We didn't want to get off at the fire floor because the smoke or the fire could be right in front of us as the doors opened. We put on our facepieces just in case; you never knew what would happen in these elevators. Cockroaches lined the ceiling and walls. No one leaned against the wall, and I looked carefully at the facepiece before I put it on. I didn't want to find a cockroach inside at some point when I couldn't get it out. As I looked around at the other guys, I couldn't help thinking they looked like astronauts, tanks strapped to backs and facepieces emitting odd breathing sounds, taking the elevator up to the launching pad.

The doors actually opened at the eleventh floor, one point in our favor. We wheeled the high-rise kit out and down to the stairwell, through the smoke door and up one flight of stairs. At the twelfth-floor landing inside the stairwell was the standpipe connection. I had Dave hook up the line, and I grabbed the tip. With Bobby right behind me, we headed through the smoke doors and down the corridor. There was no smoke in the hallway, which seemed strange. With all that fire showing in the window, some smoke had to have made it into the corridor.

"It's over here, Lieutenant," Bobby said. A policeman was standing in front of an apartment door about fifteen feet down the corridor.

"What've you got?" I asked.

"You're not going to believe it."

I got to the door and looked in. There was no smoke in the apartment, either. Standing there was a Chinese man, who looked at me and smiled. Next to him was an ironing board that was tied down to a metal kitchen table. One-half of the ironing board was out the window; at that end of the board was a cooking grill, and about a foot in back of the grill, just at the window, was a still-running fan to keep cooking smoke from coming back into the apartment. It really was ingenious, but it didn't prevent me from wanting to kill the guy.

"What is wrong with you? You're twelve floors up— you could kill someone if the grill fell off the ironing board! Or you could cause a fire!" I yelled. The cops chimed in. We were all shouting, and he just kept smiling. I had the feeling that he didn't think he had done anything wrong.

Bobby pulled the empty grill in through the window and placed it in the sink. I radioed the fire alarm office, relaying as best I could the circumstances of the incident and telling fire alarm to dismiss all apparatus coming in to the address. It was pretty embarrassing to call for additional help, only to find out I could have taken care of the incident with a water pistol.

Deputy Chief Simmons was just stepping out of the elevator as we were making up the hose we had laid down the corridor. He didn't look happy.

"What the hell is going on?" he asked me. Rather than attempting to explain this phenomenon, I brought him to the apartment. The police were still there, getting information for their reports. I told how we had found the cooking grill at the end of the ironing board, which was still tied down to the kitchen table. The deputy put his head out the window for a second, and as he stepped back, he looked at the perpetrator. "What the hell did you do this for?"

The Chinese man just kept saying, "Yes, yes," nothing more.

Down at street level, we met up with Jerry O'Brien, who had been manning the pump. "Lieutenant," he started yelling as I came out of the building, "some sonafabitch threw a bottle out the window and just missed my head. I'll kill that sonafabitch if I ever get my hands on him." I told Jerry about the guy we kicked off the elevator. "Sure, it had to be that bastard," Jerry said. "What the Christ is the matter with these people? Don't they know what's going on? Are they oblivious to the whole world?"

We were repacking our equipment when the deputy came out of the building. "You all set, Lieutenant?" he asked.

"I'm all set, Chief."

"I hope we don't get any more of these runs tonight," the deputy said, as he walked up the street to his car.

"I hope not," I yelled after him.

Jerry was still talking about the guy who threw the bottle out the window as we approached the firehouse. I had to agree as I listened to him: when you stack people twenty-two stories high in man's most modern monument to civilization, I guess you do create a separate world.

We stopped in front of the firehouse, and I jumped out of the pump to stop traffic. Charlie Williams climbed down from the wagon and went into the firehouse to open the apparatus doors and push the traffic control light to red on both sides of the avenue. As the pump started to back into the firehouse, a car ignored the traffic signal and sped through the light directly at me—I leaped out of the way. Shaken, I stood in the middle of the street watching the driver speed off. This sort of thing was not a new experience for me, or the other guys in the crew, for that matter. Every time we came back to quarters from a run, especially at night, cars ran the light. Jerry yelled out the window of the pump, "You idiot!" but the driver was long gone.

As the pump backed into the bay, I followed in front. Charlie was standing in the doorway of the patrol room. "We got company, Lieutenant," he said. As I looked beyond Charlie, I could see that someone was sitting on the long wooden bench in the patrol room. When we went out on a run, we never knew whom we'd find in quarters upon our return. I tossed my rubber coat and helmet onto the front seat of the pump and looked around for the shoes I had kicked off earlier. Thankfully, the pump hadn't backed over them. The backs of my shoes were broken down so they could be put on and taken off more easily. I slipped them on and walked into the patrol room.

The man sat on the bench with his head bowed a little. He had a heavy growth of whiskers, the hairs of which were caked together in some spots with patches of what appeared to be mud. His eyes were bloodshot and sunken, and he wore a pair of mud-stained dungarees and an undershirt badly soiled with a combination of vomit, drool, wine and mud. I ignored him as I walked over to the patrol desk.

I picked up the phone to notify fire alarm that we were back in quarters. The other guys were now coming into the patrol room.

Dave spoke first. "How'd you get in here?" he asked the drunk.

"The front door was open and I jus' came in," he said, looking up. "Whadda 'bout it?" His speech was a little slurred, but he seemed to be drying out.

"What about it?" Dave snapped back. "You just can't come in here and sit down. This is a firehouse."

"I need a coupla bucks to get to the detox center."

Dave answered disgustedly, "A couple of bucks? Fer chrissake, you can walk to the detox center from here."

The drunk looked at him with an expression of pain on his face. "I'm sick. I gotta get to the detox. Come on, you guys," he pleaded. "You got a few bucks." Everything this guy was saying we had heard many times before. The firehouse was located on a main street with barrooms on all sides. Sometimes the drunks would walk in and legitimately need to go to the detoxification center, but most times they just wanted to get a few dollars to buy a jug.

"I always liked you guys," the drunk said. I asked him if he really wanted to go to the detoxification center. He looked up at me with a very sad expression on his face and started slamming his fist on the table in front of him. "I gotta go, I gotta go," he chanted.

I picked up the phone and told fire alarm to have a police car respond to our quarters. The police car could take him to the detox center. I explained this to the drunk, and he jumped up from the seat and started walking towards the door. "I ain't goin' in any police car. They'll lock me up. Fuck you guys. I never liked you fucking guys anyways," was his final, unsolicited message, and he disappeared through the door.

The rest of the night was fairly quiet. We had a run to a dumpster fire behind a housing project, and then another run up to Route 2 for a small grass fire. It was around five a.m. when the first round of bells came in: box 753. The house lights had come on, and I was slipping into my night hitch before the second round of bells came in. As I slid the pole, I heard the fire alarm operator announcing the fire: box 753 struck for report of fire at 233 Rindge Avenue. When I hit the apparatus floor, Bobby was already springing into the cab of the wagon. Charlie and Jerry were right behind me. Once again, I donned my rubber coat and helmet.

The automatic overhead doors were now going up. I climbed into the passenger seat and waited for Jerry, who was pulling the battery charger out of the side of the pump. He jumped up into the driver's seat and started the engine. We rolled onto Mass. Avenue and then made the turn onto Rindge Avenue. As we approached Sheridan Square, I said, "I hope that guy with the grill isn't making his breakfast, because this time I'll throw him out the window."

We passed Sheridan Square and I glimpsed fire coming from the window of the high-rise. I wasn't sure at this distance what floor it was on, but soon there was no doubt. I picked up the mike and radioed fire alarm that fire was showing from the fifth floor.

In an exact replica of our previous actions, we pulled into the driveway of the complex and Jerry hooked up to the standpipe in front of the building. I called off at the location to the fire alarm operator. I looked up again and plenty of fire was pushing out the fifth floor window. We slipped on our air packs and prepared for the battle.

I screwed the hose of the facepiece section to the regulator, placing the strap of the facepiece over my head and letting it fall forward on my chest. Putting my helmet back on, I reached behind me to the bottom of the tank and turned on the air. The warning bell came on, signifying air was now in the regulator. Bobby and Charlie were now coming toward me with the high-rise kit. We entered the lobby to find the elevator on the first floor; that would save us some time. We pushed the kit onto the elevator, and I pressed floor number four on the panel. As the door closed, I noticed the population of cockroaches had increased since our last ride.

Dave spoke first: "Don't they know they're not supposed to use the elevator during a fire?"

Charlie quipped, "They have their own elevator key. We don't."

It was nervous talk, an attempt to mask the fear of what might be ahead. At five a.m., the possiblity of someone caught by the fire as he or she slept was in all of our minds.

As the elevator slowly made its way up the shaft to the fourth floor, we put our facepieces on. Again I examined my facepiece for cockroaches. I knew these ugly little bastards would try to climb on us. There was a roach on my sleeve; I smashed it with my gloved hand, the body blending into my stained coat. I finished putting on my facepiece, hoping I hadn't missed one inside.

We got out on the fourth floor, found the stairwell, and went through the smoke doors up the stairs to the fifth floor. I looked through the glass of the fifth-floor smoke doors and could see that the corridor was starting to fill with smoke. I told Charlie to hook up the hose as I took the tip. Bobby had the halligan bar, a crow-bar-like tool used for forcible entries.

"Give me the water as soon as you can," I told Charlie as Bobby and I went through the doors.

We moved slowly down the corridor, checking each door for heat or smoke. Bobby was on his knees, feeling each door with his ungloved hand. He finally found the apartment. "This door is warm!" he hollered, the words muffled by his mask. I knelt down beside him, and as I did, the hose I was holding jumped. Water had come from the standpipe and filled the hose to the tip. I pointed my light toward the bottom of the door, and could see a small amount of smoke filtering out from underneath.

There was a lot of noise now in the corridor. Some of the other companies had made it up to the fifth floor. Because of the smoke, I couldn't see who they were until they were on top of us. It was Ladder Four's crew.

"Help us open the door," I shouted through the mask. Bobby probably wouldn't need any help; he weighed about 230 pounds and worked out regularly. He placed the wedge end of the bar into the jamb and pulled back, but the door would not pop. A couple of guys from the ladder company placed their hands on the bar to apply more pressure to the jamb until it finally cracked open.

I pushed on the door and dense smoke filled the corridor. Getting down on my stomach, I started to crawl along the floor. Bobby was behind me, taking up the slack line. We crawled slowly into total blackness. I yelled to Bobby, "Tell Ladder Four to open any window they can get to!" I couldn't see anything ahead of me, but I could hear something off to my left. I continued to crawl.

It was getting hotter and hotter as we moved deeper into the apartment toward the noise. Ahead of me now I could see the red. It was coming out of a room at the end of a hallway. We crawled closer to the room, and the heat made my earlobes sting. Somehow, I had to cool down the hallway, but I couldn't hit the fire from this angle.

I opened the line and aimed it at the ceiling, which helped a little. The red was not visible all the time from where we were, and as we moved closer, I kept feeling ahead with my hand. Suddenly, I felt something soft with my glove and my hand recoiled from the object. I thought it was a body. "Oh Jesus," I said to myself, as I felt again to confirm my finding. It was soft but heavy, most likely someone who had tried unsuccessfully to get out of the burning apartment.

I handed the tip back to Bobby. I was going to try lifting the body and dragging it back to the corridor door. I slipped my hands under the pile on the floor, and as I lifted, it started to break apart. "Oh shit! It's all burned" was my first reaction. I placed my hands down again, feeling it to make sure. It was a pile of rags, nothing more. Needless to say, I was relieved.

Bobby still had the tip of the hose, and we both inched toward the entrance of the fire room. He directed the flow of water up at the ceiling first and then down toward the red glow. As the water struck the red, the room darkened. The walls and ceiling were concrete and there was no ventilation, turning the room into an oven. The heat built up and stayed there. We were lucky that the window in the fire room was broken before we got there.

Bobby kept hitting the fire and cooling down the room, enabling us to move closer to the seat of the fire. We could see what was burning: a pile of wooden furniture in the center of the room. The natural light filtering through the window from the day's dawning mixed with the artificial glow of the wheat lights being brought into the apartment to illuminate the blackened walls, now steaming from the cool water beating against them.

Deputy Chief Simmons entered the room and walked over to me. "Lieut, was the door open when you got here or did you have to force entry?"

"We had to force entry," I responded.

He looked around. "Nobody in the apartment? Did you see anybody in the corridor when you got here?"

"Nobody."

"Well, don't let the guys touch anything up here until I find out what's going on." The deputy went out into the corridor where the resident custodian was standing and asked him who lived in the apartment.

The custodian answered, "No one lives there. We evicted the tenants about a week ago. We had a lotta problems with them so we finally kicked them out." The deputy radioed fire alarm to have an arson investigator respond to the location.

I went over and told him that we were going to make up the line and drop our air packs in the corridor while we were waiting for the arson investigator. I stepped out into the corridor and walked down to the elevator bays, loosening the straps on my air pack and slipping them from my shoulders; it felt as if I were carrying an elephant on my back all this time. I dropped the tank to the floor. Worn out from the fire, I sat down with my back against the wall and my face pressed into my knees. I didn't care now if the roaches climbed on.

I thought about what Jerry had said about these people being oblivious to the world. Our continuous responses to this building, day after day, night after night, were getting close to intolerable. We had responded over twenty times this week alone, and the frustration all of us felt was reaching a dangerous level. Then I thought about the frustrations of the people who lived in the building. We were often used as a wedge against management to get basic services. When tenants did not receive any response from the management to problems in the building, they would make an emergency call to the Fire Department. To get the elevators fixed, they would say someone was trapped inside—they would get instant response and the elevator would work again. If they were not getting enough heat or there were considerable delays in getting heat, they would report smoke coming from the boiler room, thus getting both the Fire Department and management to respond. The list of these services goes on. We ended up responding to many unnecessary calls: from smoke coming out of chimneys to water leaks.

The man who had tried to get on the elevator with us had allowed his frustrations to get out of control and take on a destructive bent. I thought about tenants I had seen in the lobby waiting for an elevator with vacant stares, allowing the sustained aggravation of living in this building to force them into an emotional insulation of defensiveness that made them passive recipients of whatever came at them. Even the drunk who came to the firehouse earlier had used alcohol as his barrier between himself and his emotions and to increase his alienation from family and friends. I guess many times we were allowed to become part of their peripheral world, and at other times we were only unwelcomed visitors, entering their private world at our own peril. I leaned back and rested my head against the concrete wall.

White horses, broad-chested, running, heads stretched forward, breathing heavily through large nostrils, a fireman with large hands pulling back on the long leather reins, his face showing the strain of the ordeal. . . .

I wondered what those firemen would have thought if they were sitting down next to us now.

···*TWO*·····························

Help me! Help me! My mind was screaming, but I couldn't speak. I could see the shadow of someone in the room with me. I tried to lift my arm to signal, but it wouldn't move. I was gagging and I was going to choke to death if someone didn't remove the plastic airway from my throat. Help me! I thought I heard a sound in my throat as I slipped back into unconsciousness. Then, the light grew brighter and brighter, and two faces were looking down at me. "You're doing alright," I heard a voice say. I tried to make out the faces, but they were distorted. I could feel the pain now. My back, it was my back. I passed out again.

I pulled onto the hot top driveway behind Engine Four. It didn't feel as if I had been out of work for six weeks. I had lived in pain for over a year, trying to avoid a back operation. I had heard every horror story about back operations that a person could hear. I went to every orthopedic surgeon I could find that year, trying to find one who shared my philosophy of a surgery-less cure for a herniated disk. I finally found a neurosurgeon who didn't want to operate—he instantly became the physician of my choice. I probably would still be disabled now if it hadn't been for that two-alarm fire.

"They're striking a second alarm!" Bobby Rinaldi yelled from the patrol room. It was two a.m. and it was only a couple of minutes since the box alarm had come in. It was a nightclub on Fresh Pond Parkway. We were the first-due engine company on a second-alarm response. "We have fire showing from the second floor of this two-story wood-frame building" was the message from Engine Nine, the first company to arrive. Black smoke filled the street and billowed into the air.

"There's not many hydrants in this area," Jerry O'Brien said as we pulled onto the parkway.

"Grab what we can," I told him.

The closest hydrant ended up being fifteen lengths of fifty-foot hose down the parkway. There was plenty of fire coming out the second floor windows. The wind had shifted, and the alley we were in was now filled with thick, black smoke.

"We better get our masks on or we'll get wiped out right here in the alley," I told Charlie and Bobby, whom I found back at the wagon. We took the masks out of the alley and away from the smoke. It felt good to suck in fresh air. I gingerly started putting the tank on my back. The pain was steady, but tolerable.

Deputy Chief Simmons came over to us. "Lieut," he said, "I got a ladder company coming in the alley right behind me. I want you to take your crew inside once the ladder company opens the back for you. Engine Nine says there's a lot of fire over the stage area and they can't get to it."

The ladder company was already removing the large planks on the back of the building when we moved in. There was enough room now to get through. I crouched down and put my head through the opened area, feeling the surge of water coming through the two-and-a-half-inch hose. The fire was a tremendous red glow overhead. I moved slowly through the opening with the tip to my chest. As I crawled along the floor, the pain in my back was excruciating. What the Christ am I doing here? I thought to myself. I'm going to kill myself and the rest of the guys.

Bobby Rinaldi and Charlie Williams were on the line, Bobby right behind me and Charlie backing him up. "I can't get a shot like this," I yelled through the mask to Bobby.

"What do you want to do?" he shouted back.

"Move back down the line. I have to get on my back to get a shot."

The fire was right over the stage area, almost straight up from where we were. I opened the tip and the water sputtered and roared, straight into the air. The fire crackled as the tremendous pressure of the water smashed against the inner roof. Hot water returned with hot ash and burning embers. I could feel the hot water on my neck as I rolled over to protect myself. I started crawling away from the stage. I had to get to another angle or we would be scalded by the returning hot water.

On my stomach now, I directed the line into the ceiling. "Bobby, take the tip." Bobby moved up on the line, with Charlie right behind him. "I'll back you up," I told him. I couldn't hold the tip any longer, the pain was too great.

The fire finally under control, we were faced with lines all over the alley and into the parkway. I knelt down to brace the hose at the couplings and found myself on my knees. I was helpless. I started to roll the hose, and Bobby Rinaldi and Charlie Williams came over. They knew what was going on. "We'll make up," Bobby said.

When you become a firefighter, you soon learn that you must depend on your fellow firefighters for your life. During the course of a firefighter's career, he will get trapped many times; his breathing apparatus will malfunction or get hung up on falling ceilings; he will be injured and maybe immobilized from that injury; and he will get burned and may have to be pulled from burning buildings. Each firefighter has that special faith that a hand through the darkness will reach forward to help.

I couldn't allow myself to go on like I had been. It was apparent from this fire that I was doing an injustice to my crew. The next morning I called the neurosurgeon, and two days later I was in the hospital for the operation.

The one thing you can count on when you get back to work is that absolutely nothing will have changed. The last big change to happen in the firehouse was the horses were taken out, although they tell me you can sometimes hear the sounds of the horses late at night, whinnying and stampeding out of the firehouse onto the street.

The firehouse was my first assignment as an officer. Engine Four is located about a quarter of a mile from Harvard Square, but unlike the Mardi Gras atmosphere of Harvard Square, this district is made up of endless rows of glass-front stores, with wood-frame residential units above them. The stores run up and down on both sides of the street like giant walls, hiding from the probing eye of passers-by man's contributions to society: the subsidized high-rise apartment houses, the brick housing projects, and the mixed industrial plants, including a few chemical plants. Engine Four sits right in the center of this district and is one of the busiest engine companies in the city.

Tonight was one of those hot, muggy nights when you try not to move because the slightest effort seems to sap the energy right out of you. Engine Four had just returned from washing down a gasoline spill from the leaking tank of an automobile. The phone was ringing, and we hadn't had a chance to put our gear on. Charlie Williams was in the patrol room, picked up the phone and took the message. He looked at me, rolling his eyes as he wrote down the location of the incident. Charlie's facial expressions were always the tip-off to what was going on; I surmized that this call was going to be out-of-the-ordinary. As he hung up, he said, "They're getting calls from people on Loud Street about some strange smell in the air."

"A smell of what, Charlie?"

"They didn't know," he said. "Just some strange smell."

I hated this type of call. We were expected to ride up and down the street with heads out the windows like periscopes, sniffing the air. We had to determine what the odor was, if in fact there was an odor; usually there wasn't one by the time we got to the location and tracked down where it had been coming from. We didn't even have time to exchange greetings with the crew going off.

We could smell the odor before we hit Loud Street. Because of the heat and humidity, the odor was really offensive. The smell hung in the dead air. There was no trace of smoke or steam, but there was no mistaking the odor; it smelled just like mothballs.

"It must be coming from the Rate Chemical Plant," I said to Jerry.

Jerry looked over at me. "I hope so," he said smiling, "otherwise it's one big sonafabitch of a moth." Jerry's sense of humor often made a serious situation tolerable. Unfortunately, this was not one of those times. We could only surmise what chemical it might be, if it was a chemical at all, and we didn't know if in the next ten minutes we would be evacuating the entire city because of the threat—I had no sense of humor.

I thought about how terrified people were today about the threat of nuclear destruction. Little did they realize that the dangers involved in the production, use and transportation of hazardous chemicals could easily lead to the same nightmare.

There are ninety million shipments of hazardous chemicals transported through our cities every year. One out of every three trains and one out of every ten trucks is carrying hazardous material. With fever-pitched industrial growth, 250 million tons of chemicals are produced every year. It is not impossible to forecast an impending disaster as a result of negligence—or simply caused by accident in the not-so-distant future.

I picked up the mike from the pump radio and reported, "We have a strong odor coming from the vicinity of the Rate Chemical Company. I think it is naphthalene. Strike a box for this location." Naphthalene was a chemical I was familiar with, a white crystalline substance that when vaporized gives off toxic fumes thought to attack the kidneys. Striking the box would bring more help immediately. It might become necessary to evacuate people from their homes, and I didn't want any delay if I needed help.

We drove close to the chemical plant's main building. The plant took up half a city block. The white stucco finish of the exterior walls were cracking from the years of exposure to harsh winters. The walls were illuminated by large spotlights and the soot-stained brick chimneys extending from the roof of the plant made the building look like a large oil tanker that had run aground in stormy seas. I looked around the outside for possible vapor clouds or people evacuating the building. No signs of life.

We had to enter the bowels of the floundering "tanker." I told Jerry to put on his air pack and meet me at the back of the wagon. Charlie and Bobby were already out of the wagon and strapping tanks onto their backs. Bobby asked as I approached, "What the hell are we getting into this time, Lieut?"

"Who the hell knows?" I told him. "I think it's naphthalene, but that's just a guess."

I finished strapping the air tank on my back and started towards the steel-cased entrance to the plant. Just outside the door I stopped and told the guys to put their facepieces on before we entered the building. I adjusted the straps on my facepiece as tightly as possible to prevent any seepage of the possibly toxic gas. As tight as you could get the straps, there was always a little leakage into the facepiece.

I forced the latch of the door up and pulled on it slowly, unsure of what we would find on the other side.

An obscured light barely illuminated a large, open room, in which were two stainless steel vats at least two stories high. The outer shells of the vats were covered by a strangely colored film, the accumulation of various chemical formulas over the years. Metal stairs led up and around these vats onto open-work steel platforms; the steady roar of a venting system and the sounds of metal clanking overhead made us feel as if we had entered the engine room of the giant tanker.

We moved quickly to the far side of the building and took the metal stairs to the first catwalk, traveling across it to another set of metal stairs leading to the mouth of the vats. Looking down, we could see some forbidding liquid mixing and fermenting below us.

Leaving the mouth of the vats, we found another catwalk and another steel door. I hoped this door would lead us to a human form, maybe even some answers. The noise of the machinery suddenly increased, and we quickened our steps toward the steel door at the end of the catwalk. As suddenly as the noise had increased, it stopped. The only sound was the intermittent clanging of metal caused by the expansions and contractions of the pipes. Like a burglar, I knelt down next to the steel door and placed my light on the metal slats of the catwalk. I lifted the metal latch upward and pulled gently on the door—it swung easily outward, just enough to allow a glimpse into the lighted hallway. I could see doorways opening off a long corridor.

We made our way down the corridor looking for signs of life. It wouldn't have done us any good to call out through our masks, no one would have heard us. Suddenly a man stepped out of one of the doorways. He scared the hell out of me, and I am sure the image of the four of us in masks and helmets took a few years off his life as well. He was wearing no protective gear, only a soiled undershirt and a pair of dungarees.

Seeing that he was in no distress, I pulled my mask off. "What the hell happened here?" I asked him. "The whole neighborhood is filled with the odor of naphthalene."

"I don't know anything about any naphthalene," he shouted back at me. As I moved closer to him, I could see that his eyes were bloodshot and when he spoke, I noticed a little slurring. The sonafabitch is drunk, was my first thought, but the witches brew he was mixing might have had the same effect on him.

"Where the hell is the night supervisor?" I asked him.

"There is no supervisor on tonight," he said, "just another guy and myself."

"Well, get someone on the phone—I want to know what happened here."

"I already told you, nothing happened here."

"Well then, you wouldn't mind if I talked with your supervisor."

"I don't want to disturb him."

At that point I had lost my patience. "Either call your supervisor, or I'll have a police car pick him up." Reluctantly he walked over to the phone. He made contact with someone, but I wasn't sure who because before I could get to him, he had hung up the phone.

"Mr. Chisolm is on the way over," he told us.

The Rescue Company was calling me over the portable radio. "Lieutenant, what's your location?" Bobby Ranstrom, the captain of the Rescue Company, asked.

"We're up on the third floor," I answered.

"Do we need masks?"

"No, all clear. You won't need a mask."

We walked around the building—soon joined by the Rescue Company—and searched for clues to what might have happened. Not being chemists left us with a distinct disadvantage. Even if we saw what we were looking for, we probably wouldn't know it.

Deputy Chief Simmons arrived about the same time as the representatives of Rate Chemical did. I explained to the deputy what I thought it was, and Bobby Ranstrom looked it up in his hazardous chemical identification handbook. "Naphthalene is a white, crystalline, toxic material," he told the deputy.

"Any smell inside the building, Lieutenant?" he asked.

"Not of naphthalene," I told him.

The representative of Rate Chemical was talking with the guy in the soiled undershirt. As the deputy approached, he stopped his conversation and moved toward him. "Hi, Chief," he said amiably. "I'm Don Chisolm, safety engineer for Rate. I was just talking with one of our employees and he told me that a little of our product vented to the outside accidently about an hour ago. No problem now," he went on hurriedly. "Everything's working fine."

"Well, what about the product that vented outside?" the deputy asked.

"That'll clear and dissipate into the atmosphere." Then in a language used only when one wants to obscure the truth, the engineer reassured us that there had never been any danger at any time. I looked over to where the guy in the soiled undershirt stood and thought to myself, no danger? This idiot allows vapors of a toxic chemical to vent on a community unaware of what is taking place—in a twinkle of an eye, he might have reduced the population, and this engineer with his big smile is explaining that no one was in any danger.

Many times in my career as a firefighter in Cambridge I have faced situations that loom ominously before all others. During a chemical incident, a single error in judgment could result in catastrophic circumstances. This put us under a bit of pressure.

Incidents involving hazardous materials are steadily increasing. All too frequently, we read and hear about chemical accidents and the subsequent evacuation of communities in this country. In the last ten years alone, hundreds have died and thousands have been injured in chemical transportation accidents. It wouldn't surprise me to see chemical detection devices in some communities in the near future, and even gas masks become as mandatory as seat belts in some states.

But the biggest problem facing us when it comes to chemicals in this country is moral in nature. It seems as though we can only safely dispose of harmful chemicals at the risk of economic disaster. The other—and I think better—alternative is to force the government into a realistic regulatory system which would control chemical storing, shipping, and production, a system which would give local authorities the funding and manpower needed to identify and regulate these chemicals.

It wasn't that long ago when I was on the Rescue and we had a similiar experience. We were called out one night to the Harvard Yard to find a prankster had pulled an alarm in one of the dormitories. When we pulled into the Yard the dormitory was being evacuated. We were met with loud cheers and jeers from the students as we drew nearer.

Twenty minutes later, we were back responding to an alarm on the same campus for an experiment that had gone sour in one of the labs. Smoke was pouring from a room in a sub-basement. We had already put on our masks in the back of the Rescue before we got to the stairs. As we descended, we were met by maintenance people. "We don't know yet what the experiment consisted of. We're trying to get a hold of the guy now," one of the men told us. As we moved towards the room where the experiment had set off the alarm, the maintenance man told us that someone with more expertise was on the way.

At the bottom of the cement ramp was a smoke door, and through the glass I could see a light amount of white smoke. A young man with glasses and long brown hair came through the doors with one of the maintenance men, who introduced him to the deputy.

"What kind of experiment have you got going here?" the deputy asked.

The man answered with a little reluctance and a disclaimer, "Well, it's not just my experiment; it's a joint project."

The deputy walked beside him as they passed through the smoke doors. We followed, helping Engine One stretch its charged line into the corridor. The group stopped in front of a small, enclosed glass and wood room. Isolated in the room behind another glass enclosure were two gas cylinders; white smoke was trapped within the chamber.

I tried to overhear what the guy was telling the deputy, but I could only pick up fragments of conversation.

The deputy turned and walked towards us. "He says the gas cylinders are just inert gases, and the only danger is that the heat caused by the overheated vacuum pump could cause the cylinders to rupture. Just stand by here with the hose. The motor's been shut down. We'll wait 'til it cools," the deputy said. "I hated to take his word for it, Larry, but we don't have much choice; nothing had a label on it."

We waited for the pump to cool down and the smoke to dissipate before we left. Fortunately, nothing happened.

I never forgot that incident. Fear of the unknown in these cases filters through the brain. We were locked hopelessly in a vacuum of imminent disaster, held at bay by an experiment predicated upon and designed by the same people who harrassed us earlier in the evening in the Harvard Yard.

The local fire department in most communities is responsible for enforcing the state's fire prevention regulations which deal with flammable liquids, gases and solids. The department controls the amount stored by a permit or licensing system. The fire department then monitors this system by means of an inspection program.

Unfortunately, there is no such system for the storage and production of non-flammable toxic liquids, gases and solids. There are no licenses or permits needed for storage of these materials, only federal and state right-to-know laws and regulations controlling containers and the transportation of certain chemicals. Neither are there restrictions for amounts that can be stored safely in one location, nor are there limits to the number of trucks and tank cars that can travel through your community carrying toxic chemicals. Therefore, there is no monitoring, no system of checks-and-balances, to make sure the safest possible methods are implemented.

Further compounding the problem is the fact that very few communities are prepared to deal with a toxic leak disaster. When is the last time you heard of a mock disaster drill dealing with a large toxic chemical accident? Fire departments like Don Quixote are still fighting windmills when it comes to chemicals.

I had felt a little uneasy coming back to work tonight, but that first incident had come so fast that I didn't have much time to think about it. It doesn't take long in an emergency situation to get used to working as a team again—which is vital for survival. A firefighter's first responsibility is to the public. His duties are to protect property and lives from fire and fire-related injuries. This is an unwritten trust that the public has in us. But each one of us must, without hesitation, put our lives on the line for each other. Without that special trust, we would invite disaster.

Jerry O'Brien jumped back behind the driver's seat of the pump. "Welcome back, Lieutenant," he said as we pulled away from the building. It was a great way to return.

···THREE···

I could hear them whispering and giggling in the background. I was lying on the sofa in the living room watching an old Abbott and Costello movie on television. Every Saturday morning at this time came the attack of the little people. Today was no exception. Fortunately, I knew their plan. It never changed. Omph! Larry, my eleven-year-old, was now on top of me. He was trying to slide down between me and the back of the sofa. Once there, he would put his feet on my back and try to push me off. My head was being pulled off of my shoulders by Stephen, my seven-year-old, to the cheering of Larry. "That's it, Stephen, pull!" Larry yelled as he continued to wriggle behind me.

I knew how to take care of Stephen. With one finger I touched his stomach and he was laughing as he hit the rug. Now to get the big guy off. This was more difficult. Larry was getting stronger every day. He had successfully planted himself against my back, and I reached behind me and grabbed both ankles, pulling them up and across my hips. He squirmed, but I was able to get him to the rug. As soon as Larry hit the floor, Stephen flew through the air and landed on my back.

"OK, that's enough fooling around—we've got work to do." Uh oh, the lady with the vacuum cleaner was coming through. "Let's go," my wife said. "You guys have some chores to do."

"Daddy, do something," Stephen pleaded. They wanted me to get them off of the hook.

"I can't do anything, Stephen."

Larry spoke up, "Yeah, can we go to Dunkin Donuts this morning? You promised us." It was about a month before Christmas and I had promised to take them for doughnuts and a shopping trip to Toys R Us.

"Bev," I said to my wife, "I did promise them."

"OK," she said. "Take them out, but when they get home they'll have to finish cleaning their rooms." She always said that, but I knew the rooms would be clean when the kids returned.

Up and down the aisles of Toys R Us Stephen and Larry dragged me. They were making out tentative lists for Christmas, which would change at least ten times before the day arrived.

I guess we all get nostalgic around the holiday season, and I was no exception. As we walked up and down the aisles, I told the kids that when I was a kid, my brother and I would be glad to get one present for Christmas. Most kids got cap guns in those days.

"You must have been bad boys," Stephen said.

"No, Stephen, Santa was not as generous in those days." Larry gave me the look that all kids give their fathers at that age. We kept the big secret.

I couldn't believe the variety of toys in the store—this year the electronic toys were what most kids were interested in looking at. I thought back to when I was a kid. In back of the house I grew up in was a parking lot containing a small hill. We would find an old cardboard box and use it to coast down the hill. It worked pretty well too, until the cardboard wore away from the constant abrasion. I'd tell this to the kids and they'd say, "Come on, Dad, don't tell us any more of those sad stories." I think they thought I was making it up.

Stephen and Larry stopped next to an Atari game, which a young boy was vigorously manipulating. A group of kids were already waiting in line to play, but the only way anyone else was going to get a chance at the controls was to have them surgically removed from the kid's hands.

Shopping with these guys took its toll on me. I was exhausted. I got back to the house and pounced on the sofa to get some rest because I was on duty at the firehouse that night. I had been dozing for a short time when I was awakened by the giggling and whispering. LET THE ATTACK BEGIN! The charge of the little brigade began again. They jumped me—same plan. Again and again they attacked. They were getting the best of me, and I was glad to hear my wife's voice. "Stop it now. Let your father get some sleep. He has to work all night." Reluctantly, the battle-weary soldiers made their way out of the war-torn living room to wreak havoc on some other unsuspecting area of the house.

Later, a light snow was falling when we looked out the window. The weatherman predicted just a light dusting. I hoped he would be right. Heavy snow meant that we would spend half the night shoveling out hydrants, an exhausting task, especially if we happened to have a few fires mixed in between. I started to dress for work.

Stephen was looking through the door at me. "What do you want?" I asked him. He looked very innocent standing there with his big brown eyes gazing up at me.

"How soon do I have to have this list ready to send to Santa Claus?"

"Let me take a look at the list," I said, although I was afraid of what it might contain. "Gee, Stephen, are you sure you asked for enough?" He had both sides of the paper filled out with some pretty heftily priced toys.

"I'm not finished," he replied. "I'm still working on the list, but I don't know when I'm supposed to send it to Santa."

"You have to send it two weeks before Christmas," I told him. I figured I could reduce the size of the list by that time. "Where's Larry's list?"

"I'm working on it," Larry called from his bedroom.

"Santa's going to need a bigger sleigh this year," I sighed.

I said goodbye to Bev, Larry and Stephen, opened the door and stepped outside. It was still snowing lightly. "Be careful," my wife said, "It looks like a tough night." I climbed into my car and pulled away from the curb. As I looked out the car window, I could see the dark outline of my family against the bright yellow doorway—it looked like a painting. I waved at them, but I wasn't sure if they saw me.

My crew was already in the firehouse when I arrived. Jerry O'Brien was out on the apparatus floor checking the pump. Bobby Rinaldi was putting his gear next to the wagon and talking to Charlie Williams. Captain Belden, the company captain, was standing in the patrol room. I went over and placed my gear on the floor next to the pump.

I could hear Jerry on the other side swearing out loud. This was nothing new: every time we relieved the Capain's crew, Jerry would throw the same tantrum. The pump operator in the Captain's crew had his way of fixing the hoses in their places, and Jerry would come in and change it over to his way. I was glad to see everything so far was normal.

Back in the patrol room, I could see the Captain was anxious to get out early. "What's up, Cap?" I asked.

"I gotta go to a party tonight," he said as he walked towards the door.

"Anything new?"

"Nothing out of the ordinary," he said. "We had a coupla runs today, junk runs. I'll talk to you in the morning, Larry. I gotta get home, shower and shave, and be in Brockton by seven p.m." He was out of the door and gone before I could answer him.

The last of the day crew was leaving and Bobby Rinaldi signed his name in the watch journal because he had the first night watch. Bobby looked up. "Fresh coffee in the kitchen, Lieut."

"Yeah? I'm going up to change first, Bobby."

"Those bums out in the kitchen will drink it all by that time," he said.

I walked over to the apparatus floor and looked down the back towards the men in the kitchen gulping down the coffee. "Save me a cup," I yelled down. "I'm going up to change."

"OK, Lieut," Charlie yelled back.

I never got that coffee. As I got to the top of the stairs, the phone was ringing. I ran into my room and threw my overcoat on top of the bed and my dress hat on the dresser. *"Mass. Ave. and Walden Street,"* Bobby announced over the house speakers. *"Boy struck by a car."*

I hit the pole just outside of my room, which brought me to the floor in front of the pump. I grabbed my rubber goods and tossed them into the cab of the wagon. Jerry was already behind the wheel and the automatic door was up. We pulled out onto Mass. Ave. Traffic was stalled out in front of the firehouse, so Jerry hit the siren and I hit the airhorn. Slowly, we weaved our way up the Avenue to Walden Street, as close as we could get to the accident. I jumped out of the pump. Looking back, I saw Bobby Rinaldi coming up the street towards me and yelled for him to bring the first-aid kit.

Charlie Williams was just behind him. "I got it, Lieut," he answered.

It was rush hour, and the curiosity of passers-by brought the already backed-up traffic to a virtual standstill. A crowd of people had already gathered around the accident scene. Making my way through the crowd, I took the mike from my portable radio and asked fire alarm to send a police car to the scene to direct traffic.

"Is the Rescue Company coming in on this accident?" I asked the fire alarm operator.

"Yes, Lieutenant, they're on the way in with you."

A small boy was lying in the street on his back. A young woman was beside him, blocking the view of the boy's face. As I got closer, I could see that she was giving the boy mouth-to-mouth resuscitation. There was a little blood at the corner of the his mouth; he looked no older than seven years old. I knelt down beside them.

The woman looked up into my face, her head still at his chest. "I'm a nurse," she said, a trace of blood on her lips. "He has no vitals."

"Do you want me to take over the mouth-to-mouth?" I asked.

"No, I can do it."

"OK, I'll do the cardiac massage." I placed my hand on the boy's chest, searching for the right area to start the compression. It's difficult to explain the feeling that you get when your hand touches a child who has no vital signs: to know you will have to artificially pump his or her heart by placing your hand on the chest and compressing it, and to breathe into the child's body, trying to fill the lungs with air. In ten years on the Rescue Company I performed this mechanical resuscitation countless times, hoping that everything I did was exactly right and that I wasn't doing any damage. I have seen CPR performed on people that still had vital signs, and I have seen it performed inadequately.

In the '60s when the Cambridge Rescue Company started using cardio-pulmonary resuscitation, I was trained by a physician in the proper method. At that time CPR was a little controversial. As I remember it, some physicians felt it was imperative to resuscitate with closed-chest compression, and others disagreed.

One night we brought a patient to the hospital and began to perform CPR. The physician on duty questioned us on the circumstances surrounding the incident. While we continued our efforts, he asked how long it had been since the patient had arrested. The lieutenant at the time told him that we had received a call to respond to an address, that someone had collapsed. The physician asked how long from the call to our arrival at the address. The lieutenant stated it had taken us about five minutes.

"What condition was the patient in on your arrival?" the doctor asked.

"He had no vital signs," the lieutenant stated.

"How long had he been in that condition before anybody called you?"

"Well, the woman who was there on our arrival said that her husband had gone downstairs to the bathroom, and when she didn't hear any movement for a while, she called out to him, and got no response. She called to her son and he forced the bathroom door in."

"How long did that take?"

"I really can't estimate."

"Well," the physician stated as he examined the patient, "it was too long."

He walked out of the examining room, leaving us all staring at each other. We couldn't believe what had just happened.

We understood that clinical death takes place when the heart action stops and the other usual signs of life are absent. We knew that even if the heart stops and respiration ceases, the cells of the body will live for a short time until their residual supply of oxygen is used up. Lack of oxygen to the brain causes brain cells to die very quickly, and if this continues, the person will pass on to a state of biological death. I have read some texts that give the time between clinical death and biological death as four to six minutes; others state six to eight minutes. Unfortunately, determining these times is almost impossible. As a result, CPR is often administered at the risk of bringing someone literally "back to life" who has permanent brain damage. Maybe that's why the physician walked away—we never knew.

Another time, we brought a patient into the hospital when we knew he'd been dead for at least an hour. The physician still worked for a considerable amount of time trying to resuscitate him. The physician and nurses at the hospital used all their ability and effort to bring this man back. The physician continued asking us questions, often the same questions over and over. He had failed to save a life. He didn't want to let go, and when he finally had to, he did so reluctantly.

This was at a time before the American Red Cross had started teaching CPR in its first-aid courses. I remember, as an instructor, being told that the reason the Red Cross was slow to accept CPR into their courses was that they taught to a cross-section of the population—anyone from cub scout to senior citizen— and they felt that CPR would be a difficult method to adequately teach. I never really found out if that was the official Red Cross position or not, but at the time it made a lot of sense to me.

It still does. I have seen professionals bobble: what would a seven-year-old boy do if a person on the street went into cardiac arrest and, when he started mouth-to-mouth resuscitation, the person vomited? Or how can he make the delicate determination through the monitoring of vital signs if that person is really a candidate for CPR?

On a call to a nursing home, we found an attendant performing CPR on an elderly patient. When we examined the patient, her pulse was weak and her breathing shallow; in other words, she didn't need CPR. The woman lived, but the unnecessary, crushing pressure on her chest coupled with the direct contradiction to her breathing might have killed her.

I looked into the face of the little boy as I compressed his chest. Dear God, please help this boy, I prayed. The nurse was still trying to breathe life into him. We worked frantically, afraid to let anyone else touch him, afraid to pause, thinking that maybe there was a chance, but knowing in our minds that this little guy would not see another Christmas.

Bobby Rinaldi had covered the boy with a blanket and placed another blanket as best he could under him. I kept hoping the Rescue Company would arrive—it seemed like hours—and now I knew how it felt to be the one waiting. I told Bobby to take over the resuscitation; the nurse was exhausted by this point. He did, but she would not leave the boy's side and remained kneeling next to Bobby as he kept the rhythm of the resuscitation going.

Bobby Ranstrom was the first one through the crowd. "I'll take over, Larry," he said as he knelt down.

The crew of the Rescue brought over a stretcher, and I walked back through the crowd. I hadn't noticed the cold, but now I pulled the collar of my rubber coat up against my neck. Charlie Williams was putting the first-aid kit back into the compartment on the side of the wagon. "Did they get the guy that hit him?" Charlie said as he looked up.

"To tell you the truth, Charlie, I wasn't even thinking about that—I don't know." I was just thinking of a dead little boy.

The Rescue passed us on the way to the hospital. I was still getting information for my report. The street was wet with the falling snow. I hoped the snow wouldn't start to accumulate and it didn't get any colder so the streets wouldn't freeze up.

Back at the firehouse I was still making out the accident report when Charlie came into the patrol room. "Do you want any steak, Lieut?" he asked.

"No thanks, Charlie, I had supper before I came in." Charlie and Bobby were not married and usually cooked their meals in the firehouse. Bobby was the better cook of the two. Before he was transferred into the group, poor Charlie almost starved. The only thing Charlie boasted he could cook was spaghetti, and the first night I tried his spaghetti, most of it went through the strainer. He thought that was the way you cooked it.

Bobby Rinaldi had been with us for about four months. He had taken Jimmy Perry's place. Jimmy suffered a heart attack one night when we were at an incinerator fire, but he always blamed the spaghetti dinner Charlie had cooked for him that night.

After I finished my report, I went out into the kitchen. Bobby and Charlie were still munching on their steaks. Jerry O'Brien had taken the watch desk for Bobby while he ate. I poured myself a cup of coffee and sat down at the table. I started the conversation. "You know, I took my kids up to Toys R Us this afternoon, and I couldn't believe the toys they got for kids now."

Bobby said, "Yeah, I wish they had all those toys when we were kids."

Charlie looked up. "You're still a kid."

"How'd you like it if I made you into a toy and spun your head off?" Bobby replied.

"Is that a threat?"

"No, that's a promise."

"You heard him, Lieut," Charlie said. "You're a witness."

"Shut up and eat, you dummy," Bobby yelled.

"I don't know, I think that when we were kids we had more fun. We played more games. We were more creative, most of the time, and we'd make our own toys," I thought aloud.

"Yeah," Bobby said, "I remember we'd knock down chestnuts from the trees. We'd walk all over the city looking for big chestnuts and throw cans or sticks up to knock 'em down. Then, we'd take a nail and put a hole through the center and push a string through the hole, tie a knot and have chestnut fights. One guy would hold the chestnut and you would hit his chestnut with yours; if you didn't break it, he would get a chance to hit yours. If you had a good chestnut, you could play that game for days without it splitting into a thousand pieces."

"Is this going to be a long story?" Charlie said, interrupting his attack on the steak. Bobby jumped up from the chair and lunged at Charlie, but he was already running onto the apparatus floor.

"Lieutenant, you're a witness," Charlie yelled as he hit the stairs to the second floor. I could hear the sound of their scuffing feet as they passed over us. Somewhere between the stairway down and the kitchen, they signed a peace treaty.

I walked out to the patrol room. Jerry O'Brien was watching some old-time movie on television. I didn't know how he found them, but everytime it was his pick of TV programs, he would find some old movie. Adolph Menjou was the star of this one. When you asked Jerry about any of the old stars, he could give you a complete profile of his or her life. For some reason, I never asked about Adolph Menjou.

I looked out the window of the patrol room. It had stopped snowing. The phone rang and Jerry picked it up. "Yeah, he's right here, Deputy," Jerry said over the phone. Jerry put his hand over the mouthpiece of the phone. "It's Deputy Simmons," he said.

I took the phone from Jerry. "I need a detail for Engine Eight," the deputy told me over the phone. "Jimmy Sterin went home sick. They only have two men there now, so get the detail over as fast as you can."

"OK, Deputy," I replied, and hung up the phone. "Whose turn on the detail, Jerry?" I asked.

"It's mine," he answered. "Bobby had the last one."

"OK, Engine Eight for the night." Details were a problem for everyone. We ran short-handed most of the time, and when we lost a guy it hurt. Three men on an engine company is ridiculous. One man drives the hose wagon, one man drives and operates the pump at a hydrant. That left one guy to make the initial attack on the fire. In our case, because we were a single company house and it took awhile before any other apparatus rolled in with us, it was especially difficult.

About five minutes after Jerry left the firehouse the phone rang. "*Man hit by a car in the Porter Square Shopping Center,*" was the still. When we arrived, a crowd was standing over a man lying face down on the pavement. A small pool of blood had formed next to his face.

"Anybody see this guy hit?" I asked the crowd.

A voice answered, "He wasn't hit by a car. Two guys jumped out of a car and slammed his head on the hood of that car there."

I didn't want to move his neck, but I had to see where the blood was coming from. I got down close to his head. Just above his right eye was a large gash. Blood had coagulated over his eyelid but was still oozing out of the wound.

Charlie handed me a gauze. "Gimme a couple more," I said. I pressed the gauze over his eye, carefully trying to prevent any movement of his head. With a blow like that, he could have suffered some spinal damage.

"Get me an orthopedic collar," I said to Bobby Rinaldi. The Rescue Company had now entered the parking lot and was making its way towards us. "I'll hold his head steady, you put the collar on."

Bobby Ranstrom came over to me. "What have you got, Larry?" he asked.

"Possible injury to the neck, a gash over his right eye."

"Is he unconscious?"

"No, he's conscious."

Bobby knelt down beside us. "How are you?" he asked the guy.

"OK, I guess," the guy answered feebly.

"Any pain in your arms and legs?"

"No, no pain."

"Can you feel your arms and legs?"

"Yeah, I can feel them."

"OK," Bobby said, "bring the ortho stretcher just in case." We rolled the guy over with the orthopedic stretcher on his back, supported by the stretcher.

As we rolled him over, wads of money fell out of his pockets and onto the wet ground. Tommy Clark from the Rescue picked up the money. I got a good look at the man's face now. It was Billy Norton. "What happened to you, Billy?" I asked. He looked up at me. The dried blood that had dripped over his lid made it difficult for him to see.

"It's Larry Ferazani," I told him.

I don't know if he knew who I was, but he answered, "They were just trying to roll me." It was obvious from the amount of cash that Billy had on him that there was something more going on, but I was sure he'd never tell us. Looking down at him like this, a feeling of sadness welled up inside me.

Instant memories flashed through my mind. Many times I responded to some tragedy in the streets to find the victim was someone I had known as a boy. It always gave me a terrible sense of uneasiness. I could see Billy and myself and other friends running through the streets of Cambridge, each memory in turn sparking another memory, broken bits of life, a life endlessly trapped in our youth. It was finding Billy on the street like this that shocked me back into the reality that somewhere, sometime I was unsuspectingly released from that entrapment.

Many of our experiences might have been shared by any boy in America. For example, Billy had started me on my first business: a Kool-Aid stand, the typical initial business venture. But unlike the rest of America, we had an unusual consumer: the students from the Harvard University Business School.

First, Billy had to field-test his product in the neighborhood. The Kool-Aid stand lasted about an hour before we realized we had no market. The other kids in the neighborhood either couldn't afford the drink or were looking for credit.

Billy relocated the stand down by the Charles River with the idea of selling at a higher price to the affluent students enjoying the outdoor amenities. The Charles River was supposed to be a public recreational area under the jurisdiction of the Metropolitan District Commission. As kids we thought the universities owned the river. After all, the boat houses of Harvard and MIT lined the shores on the Cambridge side, and dormitories lined the streets across from the river. We weren't Tom Saywer and Huck Finn; neither was this a paddle boat or river barge laden Mississippi. Sailing yachts and crew sculls went up and down this river.

Business was a little better, but the lure of the cold water on a hot day provided yet another blow to business—we jumped into the polluted waters for a swim. A couple of times we were chased out of the water by the MDC patrol boats while they dragged the river for drunks who, watching us as they lay in an alcoholic stupor on the shore, would jump in the water and accidentally drown.

Billy's business schemes were usually thwarted by the MDC Police chasing us along the Charles River, or the campus securities of MIT and Harvard keeping us outside the gates of the magic kingdom. During the Harvard-Yale football games, Billy painted signs and hired most of the kids in the neighborhood to direct the cars of the spectators to vacant lots and backyards in the neighborhood—quickly transformed into parking lots. This was one of the most successful ventures, but when the owners of the property caught on, again we were chased away.

"They were just trying to roll me." Billy's pleading voice brought me back to reality.

On the ride back to quarters, I couldn't help but think about Billy Norton.

Billy Norton was the least inhibited of the crowd I grew up with. He took everything to the extreme, and it appeared he hadn't changed much over the years.

When we were kids in the early '50s, rock 'n' roll had just come on the scene. In 1953 a complete metamorphosis took place in the city through music, starting with Bill Haley and the Comets. The kids in my neighborhood were buying records, putting on pegged pants, letting their hair grow out of crew cuts and greasing it back into a light bush. The revolution had begun. America's youth were growing up, breaking the rusting chains of social rules, and casting off the fear of the atomic bomb that they had grown up under. At last, we were going to participate.

The students of Harvard and MIT did not participate in our revolution. They were content to be the offspring of the American aristocracy—"the chosen." Their choice in music was jazz, and in cars the MG. We wore velvet-front shirts; they wore blue button-down oxfords.

Those certainly were the good old days, I thought as I jumped from the seat of the pump to the apparatus floor. With all their difficulties, and there were many, it all seemed easier to endure in my youth. And much harder to forget as I aged.

I shuddered a little from the chill as I took off my rubber coat, hoping the coffee was hot as I made my way to the kitchen. Bobby Rinaldi was pouring the last of the coffee down the sink. "Don't worry," he said. "I'm gonna put on another pot."

"OK, Bobby," I said. "I'm going upstairs to make out the report on this incident. I'll be back in a couple of minutes."

I sat down at the desk in my room making out the report. Billy Norton made me remember days I thought I had put away long ago. I thought about Harvard and how the students in actuality had changed along with us, if simply a little more subtly and a little more slowly. Their tastes leaned toward the "intellectual": folk music, coffee houses and poetry.

I remembered going to one of those coffee houses with Billy. It was in Harvard Square on Mt. Auburn Street. Coffee houses were located in basements in those days: the darker and dingier, the more atmosphere. A single spotlight shone on a figure dressed in black. The figure, who looked like George Carlin, sat on a barstool in the middle of a makeshift stage with a guitar on his lap. His poetry was not like the poetry I learned at St. Paul's School. It went something like, "I spit on your shoes, and your father just left." I looked around the dark room watching the students stare into space, mentally caressing each word. I felt a little uneasy because I never quite knew what he was talking about.

The metamorphosis into student activist was a slow process, but building just the same year after year, waiting for a catalyst. We didn't know then that— unlike our revolution triggered by music—a war would unleash their violence in these same streets, and the sounds of music would be muffled by the shouts of hate.

The steam hissing from the radiators brought me back to the present. I hoped the coffee was ready. I looked out the window and it was still snowing, but the low temperature kept it from accumulating. I slid down the pole to the back of the apparatus floor and made my way out to the kitchen. Bobby was sitting reading the paper. "Where's Charlie?" I asked.

"He's out in the patrol room watching some horror movie."

I poured myself a cup of the fresh coffee and sat down across from Bobby. "Well, the snow isn't amounting to much."

Bobby looked up. "Thank God," he said. "That's all we need. The deputy would have us out shovelling hydrants all night."

"Nah," I said. "He'd wait 'til 5:30 in the morning to call you to get up and shovel."

"It wouldn't be the first time," Bobby said. And he was right.

The night seemed to drag on. We didn't get another run before midnight, and I went up early to my room. I was trying to finish some of the paperwork the captain had given me.

The bells came in. I counted the first round: four-five-five, Mass. Ave. at Newton Street. I jumped up and stepped into my boots, pulling the blue sweatshirt over my head and running toward the pole outside my room. The fire alarm operator's voice came over the house radio: *"Box 455 has been struck for a report of house fire at Number 3000 Mass. Avenue."* The apparatus doors went up. Out on the street the snow had stopped, the temperature had fallen and the world had iced over.

We rolled out onto Mass. Avenue and headed toward Harvard Square. "That building's on the right side," Bobby Rinaldi said as he drove. "I'll grab the hydrant on the corner of Newton Street."

I looked at my watch; it was 4:30 a.m. The street was deserted, a rare sight. Down the Avenue, the smoke was coming out of the window of an apartment building and hovering over the street. As we approached the building, I could see a woman's upper body hanging over the window sill. She waved her hands frantically, trying to signal to anyone who could see her.

The ladder company was coming up the street from Harvard Square, the opposite side of the street from us. Bobby pulled the pump to the corner of Newton Street, almost right in front of the building. I jumped out and yelled back to Charlie Williams in the wagon that I was going to pull some line off. I grabbed the line from the bed of the wagon and handed it to Bobby, giving Charlie the go-ahead signal, and we moved toward the front of the building.

The ladder company was already raising a ladder up to the third-floor apartment. Charlie stopped in front of the building and I pulled out the rest of the fifty-foot length. Grabbing the one-and-a-half-inch line, I yelled to Charlie who was connecting the end of the hose up to the water thief: "Get in when you get a mask on. Give me the water as soon as you can," I shouted up to Bobby, who was hooking up the suction hose to the hydrant.

As I approached the front door of the apartment, a policeman stepped out from around the corner. "I tried to get up the backstairs to get that woman," he said. "I tried first to get up the front stairs, but they were full of smoke." The fire had begun in one of the first floor apartments. The tenant had escaped, leaving the door open for the smoke to travel in the stairway.

I got through the first glass door into the vestibule, leaned down and moved slowly up the two steps to the entrance of the hallway. As I reached the floor of the hallway, I felt the line come alive. Bobby was giving me the water from the hydrant. I knelt down on the top of the landing and moved into the hallway, unable to see anything in front of me. The hallway was now filled with smoke. Crawling back to lay down on the floor, I felt a sharp pain in my knee. I must have knelt on something, I thought, and began inching toward the source of the fire. From the floor, I could see the smoke coming out of the apartment and flowing along the ceiling up the stairs. The apartment doorway glowed red.

I crawled closer. The smoke was starting to bank down on me now and I began to cough. I felt a strange warmth inside my boot as I continued towards the door.

Opening up the nozzle of the hose, I hit the fire. The room darkened and the smoke banked down heavier on me. Someone was at my heels. Thank God, I thought to myself, I couldn't stay there much longer. My lungs were about to burst.

It was Charlie Williams. "I got the line," he yelled through his mask. "Lieut, you're cut. We followed a trail of blood in here." Now I knew what the warm stuff was in my boot. I reached back, got the handkerchief from my pocket, and put it down my boot, trying to find out where the cut was.

Other guys were coming in now as I crawled towards the foyer of the apartment. When I got to the front hall, the smoke had dissipated and I was following my own bloody trail to the outside. I was coughing and holding the handkerchief in my boot. Some sonafabitch had broken the glass in the inside door of the hallway, and when I knelt down, I knelt right on a piece of it.

Mary McGinnis was on duty in the Emergency Room when the police car brought me in. "Are you faking it again, Larry?" she asked.

"Yeah, Mary," I answered. "I need the weekend off. I was invited to a party."

"OK, we'll see what we can do," she replied. "They brought a woman in from that fire. She's in the other room."

"Is she alright?"

"Yeah," Mary said, "she'll be OK."

The gash made a perfect letter 'U' in my kneecap. The doctor on duty that night was an artist—he did a perfect job of sewing. Mary recommended a soft brace and strapped one on me.

"How are you getting home, Larry?" she asked.

"Oh, I'm not going home, Mary. I have to get back to the fire."

"You can't go back to the fire with that knee, Larry. The doctor is writing a report, keeping you out of work for at least a coupla weeks," Mary said.

"I'm just going back to pick up some things before I go home," I said. I was suffering from a guilty conscience about getting injured and leaving my crew. I thought if I went back, I could at least help them make up some of the equipment, deluding myself that I had the physical capability of doing anything at this point. But I thought it would ease my guilt if I just went back. "How are you getting back to the fire?" Mary interrupted my thoughts with her question.

"Joe Levitt said he'd pick me up. He's one of the cops who drove me to the hospital." Joe Levitt was an old school friend of mine.

On the way back to the fire, Joe's partner was telling me how good Joe was back in the '60s when he was working Vice in Harvard Square.

"Joe was probably the best-looking cop we had in drag those days, but you know how old age catches up with you," he joked. "Your legs start to go, pretty soon the whistles stop—it's tragic."

I could see Joe's face flush and the veins in his neck stand out. "I see you guys get along great together," I said.

Fire hoses were still tangled in the street, but the guys had already started to make-up after the fire. You could see some of the hoses were frozen solid.

"You can let me off anywhere."

'OK, Larry."

As I stepped out of the cruiser, I felt helpless. I limped over to where Deputy Chief Simmons was sitting on the backstep of Engine Four's wagon smoking a cigarette.

"How'd you make out, Lieut?" he asked.

"OK, Deputy, a few stitches. They put this cover over the knee just to protect it."

"It doesn't look good to me," the deputy said. "Why are you back here? They should have sent you home."

"I can't drive my car like this."

"Ah Christ, you're right," he said. "Well, I'm sending your company back to quarters as soon as they make up anyway. You can ride back with them." I sat in the cab of the pump, watching the guys making up the hose; because some of the hose was still frozen, it had to be laid over the entire length of the hose bed. Someone would have to ride the backstep and hold it on while we returned.

Charlie Williams drove me home. I had to leave my car at the firehouse. When I walked in the front door, the two boys were watching me.

"What happened, Daddy?" Larry asked. I could see that look of fear on his face.

"I just cut myself a little, Larry," I said.

"You're always getting hurt on that job, Daddy." His expression changed from fear to sadness. "What kind of job is that? Why don't you quit that job?"

"How can I quit, Larry? Who will support us and buy the Christmas presents?" I said laughing, trying to make him feel better.

Stephen looked up, not quite understanding. "Yeah, quit that job," he echoed.

••••FOUR••••••••••••••••••••••••••••

I pulled the straps of my airtank tight against my chest as I went through the double doors of the lobby in the high-rise apartment building. It had been two weeks since I injured my knee, and this was my first day back at work. Earlier in the day I had told the guys how bored I was staying home and how glad I was to be back.

The call was for a fire in one of the elevator shafts. As I walked toward the elevator bay, I could see directly down the corridor. There were no signs of smoke. I figured this call would be just another false alarm, or maybe some incinerator smoke was in the corridors again.

Suddenly, there was an explosion from the elevator shaft. It startled the hell out of me. I ran to the elevator bay and was surprised to see no sign of smoke. I tried to look down through the narrow space between the lobby and the elevator outer door. I couldn't see any fire in the well. I pressed my body closer to the door and looked up through the crack. There was the fire, in the elevator car itself.

I radioed the situation to the incoming deputy, and then pressed the button on the wall for the other two elevators. My crew was now coming in, wheeling the high-rise kit. Ladder Four's crew was right behind them. It didn't look like the elevators in the other bays were moving.

I hollered to my crew, "We gotta hoof it up."

"What floor is it on, Lieut?" Bobby Rinaldi asked.

"It looks to be about the sixth," I said.

"Ah shit," Bobby said, and turned the high-rise kit in the direction of the stairway. "I'll check the floors on the way up."

I started down the corridor to the stairway. Bobby turned the kit around like a shopping cart, and started to pull it over the stairs. Charlie Williams was at the bottom and helped to lift the wheels. We made it to the third floor. At this point, we were already exhausted from our efforts.

Deputy Chief Simmons' voice was now blaring over the speaker of my portable radio. "What floor are you on, Engine Four?"

I answered him, gasping for air, "We're on the third floor, coming up."

"How the hell did he get up there so fast?" Charlie asked.

"He wasn't carrying this goddamn elephant up the stairs, that's how," Bobby snapped.

I was frustrated. "The hell with this. Bobby, you pull a couple of lengths out of the kit, and Charlie, you carry the reducer. I'll carry the wrenches."

It was much easier now and we were climbing the floors much faster, but the initial romp up the stairs had taken its toll. Weighed down with the air tanks on our backs, we were crazy to even try it, I thought to myself.

The radio blared again with the voice of the deputy. "Engine Four, what floor are you on?"

"We're on the fifth floor coming up," I responded.

We got to the door of the sixth floor corridor. Through the glass we could see thick black smoke encompassing the corridor, but I couldn't see any fire. We put on our masks and Bobby and I went through the doors. We moved down the corridor toward the alcove of the elevator bay. Ahead of us, we could hear the muffled voices of the ladder company. I could hear the sound of metal hitting metal. We moved toward the sound.

As we got to the alcove, I could see fire dancing out the top of the elevator and lapping against the ceiling. Ladder Four was forcing open the outer door to the shaft. They released the doors, and now the flames increased. It was dark in the building, the only light coming from the fire above our heads. I could feel the hose fill—Charlie had turned on the standpipe. Bobby had the tip of the hose right ahead of me.

Smoke and fire was now pouring out of the open doors of the elevator car. Suddenly I felt as if I was in a railroad boxcar, with darkness encasing me, the only light steadily dimming by the flow of water Bobby applied. There was no ventilation in these concrete structures, and the heat was almost intolerable. Fortunately, someone took out the window at the end of the corridor and gave us a little relief.

Bobby continued to pour water into the darkness in the direction of the elevator. I wondered what we would find inside. It wouldn't surprise me to find a burning body.

I told Bobby to shut down the nozzle. The smoke had now dissipated and with the hand lights of Deputy Chief Simmons and Lieutenant DiCenzo you could now see the elevator car. It was tilted inside the shaft—absolutely incredible. In the back of the car were the remains of a box spring and mattress. The ceiling light and interior walls of the car were blackened by the fire and melted beyond recognition. The cable above the elevator car was also melted and had broken away from the car. The explosion I heard coming into the building was actually the car smashing against the sides of the shaft as it fell two floors. The safety brakes were released by the friction of the falling car.

Who the hell would have done such a thing? At first I got angry—angry at everyone who lived in the building —then I started to rationalize. Was it vandalism or was it an act spawned by frustration? How many times had I entered this building to find the corridors fouled with incinerator smoke, the product of a defective system? How many times had I come in to this building to extricate people trapped between floors in the elevators? Elevators plagued people in high-rise buildings. I'd often find that only one elevator was working when we came to this building for a fire or false alarm. You'd find a crowd of people in the elevator bay standing there, some holding their childen's hands, others holding groceries, all looking up with desperation at the lighted indicator panel over the elevator doors, as if hoping against hope.

They all lived in this brick tower of isolation. The elevator becomes a vehicle to take them to the even more restrictive isolation of their own apartments, square concrete booths.

We finished cleaning up the equipment outside the building and Deputy Chief Simmons dismissed us. On our return to quarters, Bobby Rinaldi said he would finish making the breakfast we had left when the box came in. I went upstairs to wash up and make out the report on the fire.

I also had to make out a sick report on Jerry O'Brien. Jerry had called the deputy in the morning and was not going to report to work today. Deputy Chief Simmons said he didn't have another guy on duty that he could send us, all the crews were running on three men. These days we were lucky if we had four men assigned to a piece. For the last fourteen years, we had always had five men assigned, but because of budget constraints, fire departments all over the country were suffering a reduction in forces.

I could never quite come to grips with that concept. The public was never given a true evaluation of the possible consequences of a reduction of protectional forces in their community. In all the shouting, the truth usually was masked.

Massachusetts fire departments were particularly hard hit because of the enactment of a new tax law— Proposition $2\frac{1}{2}$. Real estate taxes were high and spiraling upward every year. In an effort to stop this continual increase, a group of people placed on a state referendum a limiting tax provision. Proposition $2\frac{1}{2}$ won overwhelmingly in the state's elections. Cities and towns were now limited to a real estate tax hike of no more than two-and-a-half percent a year.

This limitation meant that city and town governments were forced to adhere to strict budgets and cut back on many of the services formerly provided. The first defense of many of the local governments was to cut essential services: first fire and police, then public works and schools. This would effect the public-at-large immediately, and the government thought that this might reverse public opinion of Proposition 2½. It didn't. As a result, many of those essential services would never be the same.

I could see this in action in the Fire Department. We would never again see five men on a piece of apparatus, which is absolutely essential for a piece to adequately respond to an emergency, according to the National Fire Protection Association and an official study by the Federal Government published as a book, *Is America Burning?* But I can tell you that if you do not have an adequate number of men, it will cost the public more. Not only does it increase the threat of death or injury to the public because of the lack of manpower, but it also increases the threat of death or injury to the firefighters, which will cost the taxpayer in firefighters' death and disability payments. Somber thoughts, but ultimately true.

Emergency medical services by the municipalities during this time would not be excluded from budget cuts, unfortunately, at a time when emergency service was beginning to expand and improve again. Emergency medical service in this country made great strides during the late '60s and early '70s with the inception and proliferation of the Emergency Medical Technician programs. Before these programs, many communities used funeral cars to respond to and transport victims of accidents, often with personnel who had no training in any level of first aid. Through mishandling, thousands of accident victims were further injured, paralyzed or even killed. It's a horrifying thought, and it's hard to envision something like that today.

It will be just as horrifying years from now to think that medical services stagnated not because of a lack of knowledge, equipment or personnel, but because of budget constraints. If you or your family were trapped in a building, you certainly would pay any amount to have the best trained, equipped and prepared fire department arrive. Unfortunately, we all tend to think the same way—life insurance is only good when you get paid off. Paying for an intangible over the years is *difficult*. After all, you may never need the fire department to respond to your house.

Bobby Rinaldi's voice came over the house speakers: *"Come and get it."* Breakfast was ready: bacon, eggs, homefries and pancakes, all for a dollar.

"I don't know how you can keep the price so low," I said to Bobby.

"He steals the eggs," Charlie explained.

Bobby didn't even flinch. "I'm glad someone appreciates the cooking and the price."

"Who's on patrol?" a voice called from the apparatus floor. It was Joe Donovan, a Cambridge cop.

"You are," Charlie yelled back, and headed out with his plate to the patrol room.

Joe Donovan came into the kitchen. "Want a cup of coffee?" Bobby asked.

"No thanks, Bobby. I just had a cup before I came."

"Who'd you rip off?"

"I made Cliff buy this time." Cliff was his partner. "When does Johnny Rocca come in?"

"He'll be in tonight," I told him.

"I got another Italian joke for him."

"Oh Jeez," Bobby said, "are you gonna get him upset again?" Those two guys would swap joke-for-joke. "OK, what's the joke?"

"Well, it seems that during the Second World War there's a dog fight over Italy between an Italian pilot and a German pilot. The German pilot shoots the Italian pilot down, and as the plane heads toward the ground, the German pilot, in a gentlemanly gesture, passes by the Italian plane and renders its pilot a salute. As he salutes, he looses control of his plane and crashes. The Italian pilot crawls out of his plane and over to the German's burning plane to save this gentlemanly officer.

"The German pilot is brought to an Italian hospital, and about two weeks later the Italian pilot comes to visit him. The Italian tells him that he has bad news: the German is going to lose a leg because of the burns he suffered in the crash. The German is distraught and asks the Italian if he can do him a great favor. The Italian agrees. The German says, 'Take my leg, fly over the Rhineland and drop it. I want my body to stay in my country.' The Italian looks puzzlingly at the German, says how strange the request is, but agrees.

"About two weeks later, the Italian pilot again visits the German pilot with more bad news: he is going to lose another leg. The German again appeals to the Italian to take this part of his body and drop it over the Rhineland. The Italian is again reluctant, but agrees.

"Finally the Italian pilot visits the hospital with more bad news. He tells the German pilot he is going to lose an arm. The German is really upset this time and again asks the Italian to drop his arm over the Rhineland.

"The Italian now gives the German a suspicious look and says, 'Tell-a me something, are you-a trying to escape?' " We all broke up.

"That'll get Rocca," Bobby said, "but he'll have a better one."

The phone rang and Charlie answered it. We waited for the message. His voice came over the house speakers: "*Walden at Mass. Avenue, report of fire in the women's health club.*" It was almost across the street from us. We pulled out onto the Avenue and headed toward Walden Street.

As we approached, I could see some women running out of the health club, arms folded, trying to protect themselves from the cold. They lined up in the street, some wearing sweat-shirts over leotards, others wearing nothing but high-fashion body suits.

I told Bobby to take the hydrant at Clark Street. He pulled the pump over to the curb and in front of the hydrant. I jumped down and signaled Charlie Williams to pull in front of the pump. We could lay right into the front of the building.

I told Charlie I was going in to find the fire and that I would be right back. I passed the shivering chorus line on the street, and as I got to the front door, a girl in a blue body suit was coming out. I asked her where the fire was; without stopping, she pointed inside and replied, "In the sauna room."

I passed through the front door into the lobby. This club was originally a movie theatre and little change had been made to the structure itself other than removing the movie screen and seats. I opened the inner set of doors and looked across the red-carpeted gym floor. Along the walls were mirrors and in front of the mirrors were exercycles and weight equipment. There wasn't any smoke yet.

I knew the sauna was in the sub-basement because we had inspected this place a couple of months before. I ran toward the stairway along the right wall of the gym, about twenty-five feet away, and descended the stairs to the basement area. Still, I saw no smoke. With a quick glance, I looked over the room and then started down to the lower basement where the sauna and steam rooms were located.

I moved down the stairs and into the now clearly visible smoke, crouching down to get underneath it. I wanted to find where the seat of the fire was. Making my way slowly down the stairs, I could see the smoke getting thicker and traveling up the stairs a little more rapidly now. I didn't want to get caught down here without a mask, and I was already coughing from the smoke, so I quickly returned up the stairs.

But I had let too much smoke get behind me, forcing me to follow the walls out of the club. I could feel the pressure of the smoke at my back, filling my lungs. Choking, I felt along the wall like a blind man, trying to find my way out. I bumped right into Bobby Ranstrom.

"What have you got?" he yelled through his mask. I couldn't answer him. I pulled him with me toward the ramp at the doors that would lead me out to the sidewalk. He knew I was in trouble and kept close as I made my way through the doors and into the fresh air. I coughed and hacked and kept gasping for air. "There's a fire in the sub-basement, Bobby," I finally managed to choke out.

Charlie Williams was now moving to the front door of the theatre with the one-and-a-half-inch line. As other firefighters blocked open the doors, smoke poured out. I went over to the wagon and pulled out my Scott air pack. Bobby Ranstrom, Charlie Williams and two other Rescue guys were moving into the theatre.

I grabbed the straps over my shoulders and pulled up on them, locking the tank higher on my back. I took the facepiece and screwed in the hose to the regulator. The women had moved to the other side of the street. Deputy Chief Simmons was now crouched down at the entrance of the theatre. Black smoke was pouring out of the doors into the street.

I approached the deputy. "What have you got, Larry?"

"There's a fire in the sauna room," I told him. "One of my guys is with the Rescue and I'm going in." I passed by him and re-entered the building. It was completely darkened from the smoke. I crouched down and felt along the line Charlie had taken into the building, using it as my guide into the inferno.

Moving along the wall again, I felt for the opening to the basement stairs, stepping cautiously to find the first step leading down. The stairway had now become a black tunnel leading into the heat and fire of hell. I descended the second set of stairs, again following the line and using my foot as a cane. The concrete walls were keeping in the heat. The ladder company hadn't succeeded yet in creating any ventilation. I heard the faint voices down below and the sound of water rushing from the line.

Getting closer to Charlie, I still couldn't see any fire. Bobby said, "It's right around the next wall, but it's getting too hot down here to move around the corner. We're just trying to hold our own.''

I told Bobby that there was a door in the lobby of the theatre directly over the sauna room. I had remembered it from the inspection; the owners had blocked the door and nailed some paneling over it. It opened on a stairway leading directly down to the fire area.

"Get up and see if you can open the door. If we don't get some ventilation down here, we're going to lose the building," he said.

I climbed the stairs to the first landing. Other companies were coming down, but I couldn't make out which ones; I hollered through my mask, telling them what we had in the sub-basement. I don't know if they heard me, but they kept going. I went up the stairs to the second landing, inching along the wall and up the ramp to the inner doors of the lobby. Once there, I approached the left wall and slowly felt along it with my hand, trying to find the closed-up door.

About halfway up the wall and toward the front doors, I found the panel. I tried to pull it off the wall with my hands, but I wasn't strong enough, so I went back and found Deputy Chief Simmons, who was busy directing the Aerial Tower's crew. I informed the deputy of the situation and asked for a couple of guys from the Aerial Tower and a line into the lobby.

Lieutenant Donnelly was the officer in charge of the Aerial Tower. He and a member of his crew went with me to get a line from another engine company. Engine Eight's hose wagon was out in the middle of the avenue, and we went over and grabbed a length of one-and-a-half-inch hose from the top, pulling it over to a connection my men had set up earlier in front of the building. We hooked up the line, and opened the valve. Water filled the line.

Lieutenant Donnelly and I discussed our plan of action. I would try to find the door again, with them following me. Once I found the door, they'd have to use the halligan to pull the paneling off the wall and force the door. With the door open, we could use the line in what would now be a clear shot into the sub-basement.

Back through the front doors, I quickly relocated the panel and turned halfway around to yell through my mask to Lieutenant Donnelly. The men gathered around me, and I moved out of the way, stepping in back of the lieutenant. I could barely hear the muffled voice of the guy with the halligan telling the other ladder member to keep the line ready. Finally, I heard the sound of wrenching and breaking wood. He was through the paneling, I thought. Then without warning, fire and heat blasted into my face. I was lifted up and thrown through the air, coming down on my Scott air pack, which dug into my back. On top of me, I felt the weight of Lieutenant Donnelly.

As fast as we were flattened, we jumped up and moved with the hose man directing the line into the fire, backing the fire down the vacant stairwell. We heard the voices of the guys down below us. The pressure of the heat and smoke had been released by the door, and it was only a matter of time now until we had the fire under control.

We were in the street making up our lines. Most of the chorus line had left. I wondered about them. How did they end up here, while still vivid in my mind was the image of that high-rise building and its inmates?

How could some afford the time, energy, and money to perfect their figures, while others had to wait without hope for an elevator, their only access to their homes, to arrive?

I was sitting at my desk making out the fire report on the health club when the phone rang. I listened for a message. Bobby Rinaldi's voice came over the house speakers, "*Lieutenant Ferazani, phone call.*" I got up from my chair, walked out into the corridor, and picked up the phone. The voice on the other end was the Chief of the Department.

"Hi, Larry."

'Oh, hi, Chief,'' I answered. I wondered what he was calling me for. When the Chief called the firehouse, it usually meant trouble.

"Larry," he said, "how would you like to go back on the Rescue?"

I couldn't believe my ears. Why the hell would I want to go back on the Rescue?

"Yeah," he continued, "Jim Rowe won't be coming back to work. He suffered a heart attack three months ago, and we're looking around for someone to take his place."

What can you say to a chief when he calls you and asks you to go back on? You really don't have a choice. It was just a polite way of telling you that your transfer was coming. "Fine, Chief," I responded. "When will I be transferred?"

"A week from this Sunday."

"OK, thanks for letting me know."

"How's everything else going, Larry?" he asked.

"Oh, ah, good. This is a good house. I like working here."

"Yeah, I was assigned to Engine Four as a captain," he told me. "It's a good house."

"OK, Chief. I'll see you later," I said.

"OK, Larry," he said. "Good-bye."

I hung up the receiver. I couldn't believe I was going back to the Rescue. I had ten years there—the last two years I spent submitting transfer requests to get off. I had had enough. Every time I approached the Chief about a transfer, he would ask me to stay on a little longer because he needed experienced men. The only reason I was eventually transferred was to be promoted to lieutenant: the Rescue already had one, and when I passed the lieutenant's exam, I was appointed to a vacancy in another company. Now they got me even as a lieutenant. The Chief probably thought he was doing me favor.

I walked back to my room and fell into my chair. I was stunned. The sound of the phone brought me back to the real world. Charlie had a phone call. I got up and went downstairs to the kitchen. There was still some coffee in the pot and I poured myself a cup. Over in the patrol room, Bobby Rinaldi was sitting at the watch desk and Charlie Wiliams was on on the house phone. I sat down on the wooden bench. I don't remember what was on TV, but when Charlie put the phone down, I told them about my talk with the Chief.

The first thing Bobby said was, "Did you ask for the transfer?"

"Did I ask for the transfer? I know I'm a little crazy, but I'm not a masochist. I spent ten years on the Rescue—that's enough time for anybody."

"Did you tell the Chief that?" Charlie asked.

"Did you ever tell the Chief anything, Charlie? He was just being courteous asking me."

"Yeah, I guess you're right, Larry. Well, this means we gotta break in a new lieutenant again," Bobby sighed.

"I get transferred to the Rescue, you guys stay right here, and the only thing you worry about is yourselves," I complained.

"Who the hell else will look out for us?" Bobby demanded.

"You could have a little compassion for me."

"We do, Lieutenant," Charlie said smiling, "but we try to hide our feelings."

I got up from the bench and walked toward the stairs leading to the second floor.

"I hope you get a nice easy lieutenant like me," I said to them. "Another lieutenant won't let you get away with the things I let you get away with." Charlie rolled his eyes and Bobby just laughed.

Back in my room, I pulled the screen door closed and walked over to the cushioned chair in the corner of the room. The chair must have been there for about fifty years—even a junk dealer would have thrown it out a long time ago, I thought. Most of the furniture we had usually ended up with some kind of bug setting up house in it. I sat in the chair, not caring about the bugs or anything else, for that matter.

Memories of the hideous experiences I had encountered over the years on the Rescue Company were now returning. For so long I had kept them repressed. It was as if I was reliving the same tragedies over again. A young girl had taken an overdose of barbituates and left a note on the kitchen table telling her boyfriend why she had done it. Another young girl had swallowed drain cleaner. And still another girl was thrown through a plate-glass window by her mother's boyfriend because she refused his sexual advances. I saw their young, innocent faces staring up at me from bloodstained stretchers, looking for answers that I could not give. Once again, I felt the helplessness ... the screaming and the withered bodies of the badly injured or burned—that we could help ... the faces of little children as we took their parents from their house and out of their lives ... the drunken parents who kicked their baby down a flight of concrete stairs because they couldn't stop his crying ... the haunting look of a drunk sitting on the brick sidewalk outside the Harvard Yard who had bitten off his finger while trying to eat a sandwich he found in a trash barrel ... the friends I had known and grown up with whom we picked up in the street or in their homes injured or dead....

Blood spurted from his eyes and his ears. I had a gauze pad the size of a pillow, and pressed it down over his face to stop the bleeding. The pillow was soaked with blood. The blood was sticky and I couldn't unglue the pillow from my hands. I pulled the pillow from his face, but his face was gone. It had disappeared into the pillow. I started to scream—the sound was deafening and the bells were coming in.

I woke up with a start. I had fallen asleep in the old soft chair.

THE WAY IT WAS . . .

THE WAY WE
LIVE IT . . .

. . . The firehouse was my first assignment as an officer. Engine Four is located about a quarter of a mile from Harvard Square, but unlike the Mardi Gras atmosphere of Harvard Square, this district is made up of endless rows of glass-front stores, with wood-frame residential units above them. . . . Engine Four sits right in the center of this district and is one of the busiest engine companies in the city. . . .

... I shaded my eyes from the brightness of the sun as I stepped out onto the concrete porch in front of the apartment building. We had arrived here during the early part of dawn and had, for the most part, depended on artificial light when we first arrived at the fire. Concord Avenue was now alive with buses and cars moving in and out of Harvard Square. ...

... *We went through the bombings, the riots in the Square, the tear gas, the curfews, and the bottle- and rock-throwing for four years, degraded and spat upon by the visiting armies from college campuses throughout the country, the hippies and the street people of the time. The war ended in Vietnam, but for us there was no surrender at Appomattox, no emotional release as there was for Lee's men, who broke down and cried at the ceremony to end the war and start the peace process. The only ceremony in Cambridge was for the graduating students. They retreated from the war-torn city with their diplomas clenched tightly in their fists, leaving us with bitter and irreconcilably angry feelings. ...*

... I walked over to the window and looked out over the small Harvard underpass. White smoke was coming from the mouth of the tunnel, escaping from the exhaust of cars locked in traffic. I looked over at Memorial Hall. A few students had stopped there to talk.... The smoke coming from the small tunnel reminded me of a summer night in Harvard Square when a riot broke out and Cambridge Police had had to use tear gas on the crowd. The gas did not dissipate rapidly, and looking out of this window you could see it coming out of the mouth of the tunnel....

. . . At one o'clock in the morning, we responded to a Harvard dormitory, where we found one student running around the Yard drunk, his feet bleeding profusely from broken glass he had stepped on, and his roommate bombed out of his mind, sitting in a chair and screaming incoherently. . . .

. . . Today was moving day for me. I had just left Engine Four's quarters after spending the morning cleaning out my room and collecting my equipment for the move to "the big house"—fire headquarters. . . . If there was any redeeming factor in my transfer, it was that headquarters had many more people to talk with than the out-lying houses. Headquarters housed the office staff, three companies and the deputy chief. It was also next to the fire alarm office, so when you got bored, you could always walk over and talk with the fire alarm operators. . . .

. . . Billy relocated the stand down by the Charles River with the idea of selling at a higher price to the affluent students enjoying the outdoor amenities. . . . Business was a little better, but the lure of the cold water on a hot day provided yet another blow to business—we jumped into the polluted waters for a swim. A couple of times we were chased out of the water by the MDC patrol boats while they dragged the river for drunks who, watching us as they lay in an alcoholic stupor on the shore, would jump in the water and accidentally drown. . . .

THE FINAL BATTLE . . .

. . . I looked up the street again, and as I did, I heard an ungodly scream: "The building is collapsing!" I turned to look. It was unbelievable—no sound, no warning. This block-long, four-story building was falling. I don't know how the sound come out through my now-constricted throat. "Run!" I gasped. There was no chance of survival, no way to outrun the collapsing giant. We were going to die. . . .

••••FIVE••••••••••••••••••••••••••••••••

It had been only two days since the big snowstorm and already the mounds of snow bordering the streets were blackened with exhaust fumes and street grime. I was on my way to fire headquarters. As I drove up Mass. Ave. towards Harvard Square, I reflected on how clean the city appeared during the first snow. The snow blanketed the dirt of the city for a brief moment in time. As usual, the city struck back vehemently, turning the snow-covered beauty into hideous monuments to city life. The snow on the sidewalks was mixed with the tin cans and plastic bags, their contents exposed by hungry beasts of prey.

Today was moving day for me. I had just left Engine Four's quarters after spending the morning cleaning out my room and collecting my equipment for the move to "the big house"—fire headquarters. I didn't like what was happening, which made it even more difficult for me to make the move. A transfer from one firehouse to another is like breaking up a family. You eat and sleep at the firehouse and get close to the crew with whom you work. It is like no other civilian occupation—you have to depend on a well-trained crew for your very survival.

But I was leaving Engine Four and reporting to the Rescue Company. I knew I'd be faced with a new crew and a new role—I was coming back as a lieutenant but I had left the Rescue as a private. The crew I had worked with were no longer members of the Rescue. I had been with them for so long that, like a machine, our efforts were perfectly synchronized and we always knew what each other's reactions would be.

I pulled onto the ramp in front of headquarters and drove into a parking space next to the firehouse. I went upstairs to see Bobby Ranstrom, the captain of the Rescue, before I unloaded the cardboard boxes from the trunk of my car. The first words out of Bobby's mouth when I entered the officers dorm was "Did you ask for the Rescue, Larry?"

I told Bobby the story. He understood what the problem was, but like it or not, the show had to get on the road.

We sat for a while, and he told me how much the Rescue Company had changed since I was last assigned. "You have a full crew right now, Larry: four men. Let me get the roster for you." He walked over to his desk and pulled a clipboard down off the wall. "Your senior man is Jeff Morrison. He's been on the Rescue for about four years. He'll help you out. The rest of the guys are fairly new: Steve Miller, Bobby Foley and Andy Collins." I knew the rest of the guys, but I hadn't worked with any of them before.

Bobby went over some of the changes in procedure with me and showed me where I could store my equipment. We talked for about an hour, but as usual, a voice came over the house speaker to interrupt us, giving the location of a still for the Rescue. As Bobby jumped on the pole, he said, "If I don't see you when I get back, I'll see you Friday morning." Then, he disappeared through the floor of the dormitory.

In fire headquarters, the officers slept in a dormitory. The engine company officer, the Aerial Tower officer, and the Rescue Company officer all shared the dormitory. I would be sharing with Ted McGill, the captain of Engine One, and Bill Donnelly, the lieutenant on Aerial Tower, both of whom I knew very well.

I finished unpacking the cardboard boxes into the locker and walked down the corridor to the Rescue Company's dormitory. It was empty. I walked over to the window and looked out over the small Harvard underpass. White smoke was coming from the mouth of the tunnel, escaping from the exhaust of cars locked in traffic. I looked over at Memorial Hall. A few students had stopped there to talk.

I looked over into the Harvard Yard. The white blanket of snow covering the grass areas was still white. The Yard looked quiet. Looking out the window now, I thought about the years I had spent here at headquarters on the Rescue Company, and how many times I had looked out this same window. Those were tumultuous years. The smoke coming from the small tunnel reminded me of a summer night in Harvard Square when a riot broke out and Cambridge Police had had to use tear gas on the crowd. The gas did not dissipate rapidly, and looking out of this window you could see it coming out of the mouth of the tunnel.

The Vietnam War has been explained and examined from about every possible angle, but no one has ever explained our role in the civil war which erupted in every city in the United States, while the former occurred overseas. Everyone knows that riots took place in almost every city in the United States from Berkeley to Cambridge, but no one knows the anguish and fear that policemen and firefighters—the last defensive force in a city during civil war disturbances—suffered. In those days, the City of Cambridge had about 309 firefighters and about 200 police officers. The job of the police was to protect the 100,000 inhabitants of Cambridge against crime, while our role was to protect the same 100,000 from loss of life and property due to fire. We were unprepared to face the events that unfolded before us because of the war.

On April 8, 1969, Harvard students forced their way onto the grounds of the home of the president of Harvard. The students had overwhelmed the unarmed campus security force and made their way to the front of the president's house. They called themselves the SDS, or Students for a Democratic Society. They even had their own flag. At midnight, they read a list of seven demands. Paramount in these, masking the real issue of the draft, was for Harvard to cancel its ROTC program.

The following night, about 250 students, armed with the same seven demands, occupied the University Hall in the Yard. They would occupy the building until their demands were met, seeking to create a major media event. Unlike John Brown's attempt to take over the arsenal at Harper's Ferry, the SDS was successful. President Nathan Pusey was forced to turn to the city of Cambridge; and asked that the students be removed from the Hall.

Policemen were certainly not trained to handle this type of situation. Remember that we, the firefighters and the policemen, were products of this city. We had sworn an oath to protect the residents of Cambridge, whether temporary or otherwise.

On April 10, 1969, Cambridge Police, with the help of other local police forces, entered the University Hall with the intent of removing the protesters. The *Harvard Crimson* reported that of the 250 students that occupied the Hall, seventy-five were injured as a result of police brutality. The Cambridge Rescue's report stated that only two people were treated. The event served the purpose for which it was intended; unfortunately, we were merely pawns in their national media-attracting game. We would suffer ourselves to be "played" for the next four years.

On April 28, 1969, a threat letter was sent by the anti-war establishment to Shannon Hall, the building which housed the ROTC on campus. On May 5 at 4:30 a.m., the threat was carried out. The building was bombed, thus setting off a rash of bombings, riots and anti-war marches the likes of which had not been seen since the anti-draft riots of the Civil War. The violence continued with the bombing of another Harvard building, the Center for International Affairs, and then expanded out into the community.

I responded to the bombing of the IBM Building around the corner from the firehouse. I remember we found the fragments of the exploded pipe bomb in the ceiling on the first floor of the building. I searched around the building for any fires and found another bomb, this one intact. Standing in front of this bomb in the middle of a building, not knowing how many others were set to go off, made me a little apprehensive, to say the least.

The Fire Department would respond to 181 bomb incidents that year, up from the previous year's total of zero. As we were untrained in the art of bomb demolition, the incidents—some real and some false—had to be handled with a great deal of common sense. The Fire Department would be first on the scene and, as usual, split second decisions could save or cost lives. Many times, deputy chiefs would evacuate hundreds of people from buildings, theatres, dormitories, school rooms and business blocks. Their occupants would wait irritably outside while the deputy and his aide would search for what they believed to be a real threat.

Bombs were exploding in the city, and precautions were maximized. In one instance, a trunk was delivered to a student at Harvard's Divinity School. A University employee heard a ticking noise in the trunk, and called the Fire Department. The deputy chief and his aide hastily evacuated the building. After an exhaustive investigation of the trunk's owner, now satisfied that he was not an active militant, they removed the lock and lifted the lid of the trunk. Inside was a battery-operated toothbrush that someone had left on, vibrating back and forth. The chief laughed nervously, a laugh of relief. He would face this situation over and over and over, each time never knowing the outcome.

We would also be met with other demonstrations of the hatred the students felt against us as "the establishment." While responding to incidents in the city, bricks and bottles would come out of nowhere and hit the apparatus—and sometimes us. The city, through civil defense, was forced to place protective shields over the windshields of the apparatus and also protective housings over the tillermen on the ladder trucks. For the first time anyone could remember, we had to lock the firehouses and start all-night patrols for our own protection. Also for the first time, firefighters were requested not to wear their uniforms going to and returning from work in the hope of evading attacks by dissident students.

A seasoned lieutenant is responding to an incident in Harvard Square, one of the many calls coming in to the fire department this evening. Student militants were active in and around the city. As the apparatus approaches the Harvard Square area, the lieutenant, standing in the open cab, sees that militants have torched some trash barrels and thrown them into the street. Fire from these barrels is impinging against some buildings. The lieutenant looks over at the kiosk that serves as the entrance to the subway. Hundreds of students are amassed there, screaming obscenities at the firefighters.

Suddenly from above, pebbles are raining down on top of the firefighters, hitting them and the apparatus. The lieutenant looks up and sees that the students have taken to the rooftops. Infuriated, he is tempted to turn the fire hose, with 100 to 150 pounds of water pressure, upon these agitators. In fact, a cry from someone in the Square tells him to do it. He has to make a split second decision. These people in front of him had come out of their hallowed halls of ivy to destroy his city, a city he has sworn to protect. He knew if he turned the hose on them, he would splatter them against the wall of the kiosk and wash them down the subway stairs. And if he hit those on the roofs, they would drop like pins in a bowling alley.

The lieutenant moves forward with the hose, hitting the flaming trash barrels, keeping the fire from igniting the adjacent buildings. He leaves the barrels in the street on fire and moves the apparatus away from more confrontation. He watches the small fires from a distance, ready to move back in if it becomes necessary.

The question of the validity of the Vietnam War was being settled on the streets of America. Many of the guys I worked with were WWII and Korean War veterans. Most guys had opinions on Vietnam, but any opinions were kept private. Our first responsibility was to the public, by law and by choice. We had a responsibility to the citizens of the city and to the students of the colleges here. Many times we had to enter ''enemy territory'' to administer first aid, and sometimes we were kept from performing that task. Or we might be giving first aid to the same person who that very night may plant a bomb that would kill us—with no remorse and in the name of justice. That really bothered me.

I remember trying to draw parallels from this civil disturbance to the Civil War. I remember reading about the Civil War and trying to understand how brother fought brother and how the enemy lived across the street and looked like you and talked like you. I thought maybe it would help me sort out some of my own confusion. It wasn't until I had experienced these events that I could feel what some of the soldiers of the Civil War must have felt, but it didn't make me understand any better.

We went through the bombings, the riots in the Square, the tear gas, the curfews, and the bottle- and rock-throwing for four years, degraded and spat upon by the visiting armies from college campuses throughout the country, the hippies and the street people of the time. The war ended in Vietnam, but for us there was no surrender at Appomattox, no emotional release as there was for Lee's men, who broke down and cried at the ceremony to end the war and start the peace process. The only ceremony in Cambridge was for the graduating students. They retreated from the war-torn city with their diplomas clenched tightly in their fists, leaving us with bitter and irreconcilably angry feelings.

A rookie lieutenant is faced with an overturned and burning police car on Mt. Auburn Street. He moves in to put out the fire and is met by a student chain preventing his advance. The chanting of "Pigs! Pigs! Pigs!" grows louder and louder, until the crowd seems to be shouting itself into a frenzy. The lieutenant tries to reason with them, there may be an explosion if they can't get water onto the car soon, but he cannot be heard above the yelling. The lieutenant moves his apparatus back slowly, trying to keep the situation in hand. Moments later, the police come in and form a wedge, moving the students away from the burning car. Now, the fire apparatus is able to drive in and extinguish the burning car.

I am sure the same incidents were repeated all over the country, especially in the college towns. I know in our city, like the Vietnam veteran, the fire and police departments didn't even get a handshake of gratitude from their city fathers or the university administration, nor did the civilian government get recognition for keeping the civilian population safe when it seemed that the society was coming apart.

I could see a faint light in one of the dormitory windows as I turned to walk back to the officers dorm. I knew that the light would get brighter, and for some strange reason the thought gave me hope. Although I didn't agree with much of the students' protests or their preaching of hate at the time, I believed that it was necessary for someone to carry a banner in opposition to policies that might not be popular with the entire society: that was the essence of democracy. Student activists are these banner-carriers, passing down this obligation from class to class. But they should never carry out the responsibility at the expense of the society in which they live.

If there was any redeeming factor in my transfer, it was that headquarters had many more people to talk with than the out-lying houses. Headquarters housed the office staff, three companies and the deputy chief. It was also next to the fire alarm office, so when you got bored, you could always walk over and talk with the fire alarm operators.

Reporting to work that first night was like reporting to the Fire Department for the first time—everything felt strange and new. Although the house had not changed, the faces of the men in the other companies had. I knew most of them, but it still felt different than when I was last assigned. I went into the dry room to get my gear. Ted McGill, the captain of the engine company, was just coming out of the room. "Congratulations, Larry," he said facetiously. "Welcome back to Fantasy Island."

"I see nothing has changed, Ted," I quipped.

"Not around here, Larry," he said, as he brushed past me to get out onto the apparatus floor. I picked up my gear and brought it out to the Rescue truck, placing it next to the truck on the floor. Bobby Ranstrom was upstairs. It was ten minutes to roll call. I jumped into the cab and checked over some of the equipment.

Bobby Foley opened the door on the driver's side and placed his coat on the seat. "How you doin', Lieutenant?" he said.

"OK, Bobby."

"Glad to be back?"

"Mixed emotions," I told him. I didn't want to tell him that I disliked coming back. I was here and I had to accept the fact, not let the other guys in the crew know my true feelings. Every one of them was here by choice.

After roll call I asked the guys to get changed into their work clothes and meet me back on the apparatus floor. I wanted to start drilling with them right away. They were as unfamiliar with me as I was with them. I sat in back of the Rescue with the crew, discussing feelings about the Rescue and what we might need to drill on. Jeff Morrison, the senior man, felt we needed some drill time at the auto junk yard cutting up cars and using the extrication tools. Steve Miller thought the crew needed some work on rappelling out the window of the drill school. He hadn't rappelled for eighteen years— since he came on the job. Bobby Foley just wanted to drill on anything. He said they hadn't drilled for a long time. Jeff Morrison didn't like the accusation but let it go. Andy Collins was the newest guy to the Rescue. He had some ambulance experience before coming to the Fire Department and wanted to drill with some of the tools we used.

I got a lot out of these discussions. I watched the interaction of the crew with each other. I felt we had a long way to go to work as a unit, and we had to begin now. Nothing had changed as far as equipment and first aid techniques went since I left the Rescue. I thought we at least would be to the defribulation stage of life safety, so vital in those first few seconds of heart attack. I knew it was expensive training, but if Rescue companies were to progress with rapidly changing medical advances which had a significant effect on the population, then city governments would not be ill-advised to support this effort.

The Cambridge Rescue Company is a heavy duty Rescue. It responds to every fire incident and emergency in the city. It is proud of its tradition and success, a success made possible by its personnel drawn from the firefighting ranks. The motivational forces that bring men to this Fire Department and every fire department are what provide the most important ingredient in medical emergencies: compassion. The ten years of experience I had on the Rescue convinced me that even if you have the best-trained and best-equipped personnel, you must balance this with properly motivated and supervised people. Many times I have been asked, "After so many years, don't people who work in your field become less compassionate and more mechanical?" If you become less compassionate, it's time you step aside, because it's both dangerous and an injustice to victims of tragedy.

Over the years I have seen the effects of unsupervised and dispassionate emergency personnel. I have seen automobile accident victims dragged out of their vehicles and thrown onto stretchers with careless disregard. I have also seen unconscious or alcoholic victims, unaware they were even injured, mishandled or subjected to further injury.

The video journalist substantiates these observations on the nightly news, but is not without guilt in the matter. The camera pans the street, picking up the blood stains of an earlier tragedy. The journalist, late to the scene, tries to capture the most ghoulish aspects for his waiting audience. If he is lucky, he can make sure the camera picks up the blood-stained clump of hair trapped in the smashed windshield; or if he is really fast, he can show the emergency attendants carrying what is left of the victim, further insulting his/her dignity. Legislation to protect victims from this violation needs to be implemented.

Fire departments are optimum vehicles for administering successful emergency medical service. They are already geographically well-located, and have developed a workable communication system. Medical service is administered by highly motivated personnel who are well-trained and constantly monitored. Most importantly, the department is supervised and held publicly accountable.

The fire departments in this country should form the nucleus of well-planned emergency medical services, starting with organization under the Federal Department of Health, Education and Welfare and the appointment of fire department personnel and health care professionals from around the country to serve in this organization on a rotating basis. Responsibilities would include the development of curriculum with a national standard of proficiency higher than that which presently exists in the form of the emergency medical technician (EMT). Each state would also appoint fire department personnel and health care professionals to serve on a state-run agency of Health, Education and Welfare on a rotating basis. Their responsibilities would be to implement and monitor the training and supervision of emergency medical services—both civilian and fire department run—funded and regulated by the state and federal government.

After the drill, I went up to the officers dormitory to review some of the reports I had to make out. It had been a long time since I had made out a Rescue report, and I needed the time for review. Ted McGill was sitting at his desk when I entered the dormitory. "That was a long drill. I hope you're not going to have a drill like that every night. You might embarrass the other companies into doing the same," he laughed.

The phone was ringing before I got to my desk. I stopped and listened for the message. "*Rescue Company going out,*" the voice came up over the station's speakers. "*Four-four-four Franklin Street. Boy with his hand caught in a machine.*"

I hit the pole next to my desk, landed on the apparatus floor and ran for the cab of the Rescue. Bobby Foley was already in the driver's seat, and the overhead doors rolled up. I looked back into the rear compartment. "Everybody on," I yelled.

"OK," Steve Miller yelled back. We went down Quincy Street to Mt. Auburn, and then onto Putnam Avenue. Not only did I feel odd because the district we were in was my old neighborhood, but I still had the feeling this was my first day on the Department.

We pulled up in front of 444 Franklin Street, a six-family house. "What floor?" I asked Bobby before I jumped out of the cab.

"Top floor, Lieut."

We knocked on the door, which opened to reveal a frightened little boy gazing up at us. He looked as if he had been crying. "What happened?" I asked. He just pointed into the apartment.

We went inside and saw a slightly older boy, about ten years old, with the telephone up to his ear with one hand and the other hand stuck in an automatic cake mixer. He was crying and talking into the phone. Jeff Morrison stepped by me and walked over to the boy. He looked at the mixer, pulled out the plug and pressed the beater release. The boy's hand was freed. It was reddened from the pressure of the mixer blades, but there didn't seem to be any breaks.

"Who are you talking to on the phone?" I asked.

"My mother," he said.

I took the phone from him and identified myself to the woman on the other end. She was hysterical. "Is he all right?" her voice trembled.

"He's fine," I assured her. "We're going to take him to the Cambridge Hospital just to make sure."

"I'll meet you there in the Accident Room."

I hung up the phone and told Andy Collins to put the boy's hand in a sling. Then we could put him onto our chair stretcher.

I looked around the room as Andy and Jeff put the sling on the injured boy. The little boy who had answered the door was standing in the middle of the kitchen now, staring at us and wondering what his fate was going to be. "How would you like to ride in a fire truck?" I asked him. A smile broke out on his face. I knew I had said the magic words.

The rest of the night was relatively quiet. We had a couple of false alarms before midnight and I went to sleep playing a trivia game with Ted McGill, much to the chagrin of Bill Donnelly, who hated trivia. I think the last question I asked before I feel asleep was, what was the name of Tom Mix's horse?

It was two a.m. when the phone rang. I jumped out of bed and ran to answer it. "Lieutenant Ferazani."

"Heart attack at the Mt. Auburn Hotel on Mt. Auburn Street." We were there in minutes. I told Jeff Morrison to bring the O$_2$ box and Jerry Collins to bring the chair.

A security guard met us on the first floor of the hotel and led us to the service elevator. He didn't want anyone in the hotel to know what was going on—it would be bad publicity. We got off the elevator on the tenth floor and rushed down the hall to Room 104. The guard unlocked the door and let us brush past him.

The man was lying on his back. He looked to be no more than thirty years old. I was startled by a noise—another stepped out of the bathroom and into the room. "He got up a few minutes ago to go to the bathroom and I heard him hit the floor," he said.

I knelt down beside the man and put my fingers on his carotid artery. There was no pulse, his skin was still warm and he wasn't breathing. I brought a plastic airway out of my shirt pocket. Steve Miller was pulling out the air bag and attaching the oxygen bottle. I put the airway into the man's throat and then felt down to his xiphoid process so I could get the right position of my hand for closed cardiac massage. Steve put the facepiece of the airbag in place and started compressing the bag, forcing O$_2$ into the lungs of the man. In rhythm, he forced in the air and I compressed his chest. The raising of the man's chest indicated positive entry of the air. I told Bob Foley to take over my position on the man's chest. Bob knelt down beside me and when we were in rhythm, we exchanged places.

I asked the roommate how long he had been on the floor before he called us. He said, "I heard him hit the floor and I called down to the desk. It wasn't any more than a minute. I don't know what happened," he kept repeating. "He just went to the bathroom. We stayed in all night. We had an early sales meeting in the morning." They had flown in that night from Ohio. "Is he going to be all right?"

"I don't know," I told him, and I didn't. We moved the man onto the chair while we continued the CPR, which was incredibly difficult but vitally necessary if there was going to be any chance for his survival. As we went down the elevator to the lobby, I wondered how any less than four men could transport a victim and effectively administer CPR all the way to a hospital—it was both physically and emotionally draining. Like a machine, you conducted the rudiments of CPR, but unlike a machine, you were full of anxieties. A life was delivered into your keeping, and along with it a tremendous responsibility. The short trip to the hospital has a profound effect on all of us. John Donne wrote, "Any man's death diminishes me because I am involved in mankind." When you are so close to death continuously, those words burn into your brain.

The hospital staff was waiting for us as we wheeled the man through the glass doors of the Accident Room. Two nurses and one doctor assisted us in transferring the man from our stretcher to the hospital bed. We waited around the Accident Room for a while that night, but the man didn't pull through. My first heart attack victim since I came back to the Rescue, a young man away from home, dies in a strange hotel room. The only consolation was that in our hearts we knew we had done all we possibly could. More importantly, we had treated him with dignity.

It took me a long time to fall back to sleep that night, but before I did I heard a voice say, "What the hell was Tom Mix's horse's name?"

••••SIX•••••••••••••••••••••••••••••••••••

Spring's bright moon and the light from the tower of Memorial Church illuminated the Harvard Yard, creating a postcard perfect scene. I had been on duty now for about an hour. I completed the entries to the Rescue Company's journal and, with arms folded on the windowsill, I looked out toward Memorial Hall, just to the right in front of the firehouse.

To the tourist, Memorial Hall is an architectural feast for the eyes. The building is Ruskinian Gothic, one of the few existing buildings in this style in the Boston area. To me, the hall had been nothing more than a giant timepiece for many years. While attending high school a block up the street, I could see the clock in the tower from just about any classroom. I was in my sophomore year when the tower was destroyed by fire.

To the left of the firehouse is Memorial Church, with its white spiral tower, dedicated to the students of Harvard who lost their lives during the World Wars. Lighted on a night like this, it cast a glow over the Harvard Yard, providing almost a subliminal image.

Looking down into the Yard I could see the hastily made banners of hate. I could also see the crowd of students with their long hair and I thought how difficult it was to distinguish the men from the women. They were dressed alike, with Army surplus field jackets and bleach-stained dungarees, marching barefoot through the night and shouting anti-war slogans. Ordinarily, we were used to demonstrations in the Harvard Yard. Over the years we had witnessed "demonstrations" in the form of the panty raid, a traditional event. Once in a while the demonstrations could get a little violent. Demonstrations such as Save the Sycamores, Anti-Jay Walking and the like continued over the years, but never posed any threat to the community. But this time was different: the violence in the Yard spilled over into the streets and threatened our well-being. The increased rock-showers and bombings of the police and fire apparatus forced us to react to protect ourselves. Like the captain of a navy ship during the war, the chief of the Fire Department instituted all-night watches. All firehouses had to lock their doors and be watchful of strangers entering the firehouse. We were a community under unofficial martial law. It felt as if the country was coming apart, cracking under the stress of these successive rebellions.

Bill Donnelly, on the first watch that night, said over the house speakers: "*Lieutenant Ferazani, visitor on the first floor.*" I walked toward the stairs at the front of the building and started down, wondering who could have come in to visit me at this hour. Near the front door outside the patrol room Andy Collins was talking to a woman. I figured she had come in to ask for directions. As I moved closer, I could see that the woman had a baby in her arms. Andy turned to me and said, "I'd like you to meet the new addition to the family."

It had been two months since Andy first got the word. About eight o'clock one night shift the phone rang; it was Andy's mother-in-law. She told him that it was "time" and she would meet him at the hospital. I remember how nervous he looked going out the door. For some reason, Andy had never looked like a fire-fighter to me. He looked more like a pitcher for the Boston Red Sox—he was tall and lanky and didn't look old enough to shave. About three hours went by before we got the call—Andy was the father of a seven-pound baby girl.

"This is my wife, Stephanie, and this is little Ann-Marie," he said proudly. The baby brought an un-usual softness to the dingy firehouse. Her clear bright eyes and puffy pink cheeks on creamy white skin were amazing, and I couldn't resist the temptation to pinch one tiny cheek. I started to talk baby talk and her face broke into a smile.

"You have a way with girls, Lieutenant," Andy joked.

I retorted, "Only at this age."

The sounds of the pole hole opening and closing could only mean that the other guys in the crew were approaching. We all stood inside the vestibule for about fifteen minutes, talking and trying to get some small response from the baby. We were lucky that night; we didn't have any incidents early in the shift.

At about seven o'clock, we decided to drill with the long spinal board out on the front ramp because it was such a beautiful night. At this time of year, between graduation and class reunions, foot traffic in front of the firehouse increased significantly, and with it the never ending requests for directions and information. We never did finish the drill.

It was an exciting time of year for the students, many of them anticipating commencement day. It was strange, I thought. We had stood in front of this firehouse year after year, watching graduating class after graduating class come and go. While here, they subjected us to their whims and their causes. We protected them and responded to their fires and injuries on the streets of Cambridge and in their dormitories, but like strangers they would now pass us by.

This relationship is engrained in the very nature of the University and the Cambridge community. The community of Cambridge is mostly made up of working-class people, some of who are resentful of being excluded from the Harvard establishment, or resentful of the arrogance with which Harvard often treats them.

On the other hand, the student population of Harvard is made up of the most outstanding scholars and athletes this country has to offer. It is a university which produced five presidents and some of the most distinguished names in government, industry, and the arts and sciences. Every year these students are selected from elite private schools and some public schools, and many are descendants of former students. When they arrive here as freshmen, they meet directly across from our firehouse at Sanders Theatre. Each one knows why he or she was chosen. Each one is an individualist, a trait nurtured by Harvard. A sense of community is absent. Nathan Pusey, president of Harvard during the riots of the '60s, once said, "Harvard was here before Cambridge and is the most important thing going on in this City." This statement is indicative of the institution, offering the universally accepted attitude of the University towards Cambridge and its community.

"Rescue Company going out," I could hear over the house speakers. Bill Donnelly shouted out the still address: 675 Athens Street. We pulled out, down the ramp and onto Broadway heading toward Quincy Street. We stopped at the intersection of Dewolf and Mt. Auburn Street, and I looked out at St. Paul's Church. It had been my parish when I was growing up. We passed St. Paul's School, my grammar school, and took a right onto Athens Street.

Ahead of us we could see the flashing blue lights of a police car; we pulled up behind it. The first floor apartment door was open and we could hear a woman screaming from somewhere in the back. We rushed up the front steps and moved down a small, darkened hallway toward the sounds until we got to the kitchen.

The first thing we saw was blood—on the floor and on the walls. Two policemen were wrestling with an hysterical young woman, the source of the noise. She was struggling furiously trying to break their grip. Blood was seeping from her wrists, and she was crying convulsively. I couldn't see how bad the cuts were, but I opened up a couple of packages of four-by-four gauze. As one of the policemen held her arms, I tried to place the gauze on her wrists. She pulled away.

"I want to die," she screamed. "Let me die." I tried again to grab her wrist—both my hands were now covered with blood. One of the policemen finally secured a grip and I managed to place the gauze over one wrist. Her other arm got loose from his grasp and she flailed her arms at my back. "Leave me alone, you bastard. I want to die."

Andy Collins had brought the chair stretcher in with him and was now behind her. I tied off one wrist and held the bare palm of my blood-stained hand against the wrist of her other hand. Andy now grabbed her arms and together we placed her back in the chair. She was exhausted by this time, and so was I. I was now able to place a four-by-four gauze over her other wrist.

She had done a good job, but not good enough to kill herself—just enough to signal a need for help. The blood continued to seep through the gauze. I made two small clumps of gauze and placed them over the existing bandages. It had been two months since my return to the Rescue. I had a strange sense of déjà vu.

On the way to the hospital I asked her some questions, trying to get her to talk to me. She just stared straight ahead with a vacant expression on her face. Looking down at her, I noticed that her eyes looked dull; the dark rings underneath made them look sunken back into her head. The report said that she was nineteen years old, but she looked as if she was going on sixty. I had seen so many young women in this town attempt the same thing. We had no magic key to release them from their anxieties.

I pulled the white blanket which had slipped down over her chest up close to her neck. As I did, she looked up at me. I asked her how she was feeling. She didn't answer. Her eyes closed and her head fell forward on her chest. I placed my thumb over her eyelid and pulled gently upward. She moaned when the light struck her eye and fought to close the lid. She wanted to drift off into unconsciousness, but I kept her awake the rest of the way to the hospital.

We were in the hospital for about five minutes. Steve Miller was chiding Jeff Morrison in the coffee room. ''It's your turn to buy the coffee.'' He turned to me and said, "This guy has attack dogs in his pocket, Lieut. Miniature Dobermans."

"Aw, you still have your First Communion envelope you never opened," Jeff said to Steve. I left them arguing, and walked toward the front desk to get some information from the nurse. Passing the small cubicle in the Accident Room, I saw the girl we had just brought in. She appeared to be sleeping, lying on her back with her face toward the ceiling. Plastic intravenous tubes were inserted into her arms. The tubes spiraled upwards to plastic pouches filled with clear liquid—the familiar shapes of modern medicine. She was still alone.

When we get the call, it's already too late to prevent a suicide attempt. We can deal mechanically with the injury to the body, but we are unarmed and unprepared to deal with the problems of the mind. This added to my frustration on the Rescue, and increased my sense of inadequacy.

Box 351 was coming in as we got back into the Rescue. "That's St. Mary's Road, just up the street from here," Bob Foley said.

"Everybody on?" I yelled.

"OK back here."

We started out onto Cambridge Street, heading up toward Prospect. After putting on my rubber goods, I strapped the air pack on my back. There was an advantage to being on the Rescue: you could get fully dressed and put your air pack on inside the vehicle. As we turned on to Prospect Street, I could hear Engine Five over the radio: "We have a sofa on fire on the second floor of a three-family dwelling." We reached the intersection of St. Mary's Road and Prospect Street about the same time as Ladder Three.

The building was only about two houses from the intersection. I told Bobby to park out on Prospect Street. We could walk in. They were taking the still-smoldering sofa out of the front when we got there. I looked up at the second floor windows, open and showing some very light smoke. Deputy Chief Allen was coming down the stairs. "OK on the Rescue, Lieutenant," he said. Steve Miller and Andy Collins were just coming up behind us. I told them that we had been dismissed.

A police car was parked on the corner. As we approached, Billy Clancy, one of the cops, yelled, "Hey, Larry! We have an epileptic seizure going on in the back seat."

We ran up to the car to find the other officer in the back seat, struggling with a guy lying face up on the seat. "OK," I told him, "we got it." He climbed out of the back —he was a mess—and now it was our turn. Jeff Morrison got into the back seat. He was six foot one and weighed about 225 pounds; at that size, he was the best wrestler among us. I opened the door on the opposite side. The guy was imitating the motions of a seizure, but we could tell that it wasn't for real. He was picked up drunk by the police, and they were taking him to the detoxification center at the Cambridge Hospital. He went into his act on the way to the Center, and the officers pulled over so one of them could climb into the back seat.

"Jeff, he's acting," I said.

"Yeah, I know it, Lieutenant. What should we do with him?"

"Well, he was going to the hospital, so let's take him there." Steve brought the chair stretcher around. I yelled at Billy Clancy, pretending to be angry, "I don't mind you guys calling us for an emergency, but this is getting ridiculous. Now you're delivering them to us." Billy laughed as he pulled away. They were glad to get rid of the guy.

On the way back to the Rescue, Jimmy Thompson—that was the name he gave to Steve when we put him in the back of the Rescue—settled down. A strange-type drunk, I thought. In many ways he reminded me of our nemesis, Rodney, who used to lay on the ground in a crowded area and start moaning. Someone would call the Rescue and we would pick him up and bring him to the hospital. He lived right behind it, and as soon as we put him on the cot in the hospital, he would get up and walk home. Many times in Harvard Square he pulled the stunt. We couldn't explain to the crowd that he was a phony because he was so convincing. He weighed about 300 pounds, which made the whole thing even more distasteful. Rodney, in all fairness, didn't have a full issue. When we would get him in the back of the truck, all he would say is "God bless you boys." He never answered any of our questions.

"Well, I guess we have a new Rodney," I said.

It was nine o'clock at night when we left the emergency room of the Cambridge Hospital. I was hungry and had forgotten to bring a sandwich. I asked Bobby what he brought to eat. He hadn't. "How about a sandwich at Elsie's on Mt. Auburn Street? We could pick it up," Bobby said.

"Yeah, that's OK with me. I'll see what the rest of the guys want." Jeff had brought a sandwich from home, but Steve and Andy said they wanted sandwiches too.

Fire alarm came over the radio: "Rescue, are you available?"

"Yes, we are available," I answered.

"Respond to 321 Erie Street—heart attack."

"Rescue Company is responding," I answered and repeated the message.

We were met at the front door of the house on Erie Street by the man's wife. "He's upstairs." She was hysterical. "Please hurry, please." We rushed up the stairs to the second floor. The man was lying on the floor face down. I rolled him over. No pulse. Andy Collins was slipping an airway into the man's mouth as I began the cardiac massage.

The wife was crying, "Oh God, he's dead. Oh God."

A teenage boy came into the room. "What happened?" Tears filled his eyes. "What happened, Ma?"

"He's dead, Joey. Oh God, he's dead."

The boy looked down at us. "Is he dead?" I couldn't answer him. I told Jeff to take the boy and his mother out of the room. It was hard to imagine what people think when they see someone kneeling over their loved one and pounding on his or her chest.

The nurses were waiting for us as we entered the emergency room. We were quickly surrounded by the familiar smell, sounds and sights of an emergency unit working on a heart-victim: injecting adrenalin, delivering electrical impulses to defribulate the heart, and hooking wires to legs and wrists.

I walked away and entered the room where the nurses had their coffee, pouring myself a cup and putting it on the arm of the chair to light up a cigarette.

I thought about the teenager that had witnessed his father's death, how difficult it must have been for him. My father had died in Florida about a year ago. He got sick on the way down, so when he arrived he went to see a doctor who put him in the hospital. I didn't know anything about it until my brother called and told me that the doctor thought my father had cancer. My father had taken good care of his health. He was constantly being checked by a physician here in Massachusetts and had numerous tests right up until the time he left for Florida, so this diagnosis seemed ludicrous. I asked my brother for the doctor's number; I was going to call him, but I never got the chance. My brother called me back and told me that the doctor had called again. My father had died. The autopsy proved the cause to be pneumonia, not cancer.

My brother and I wanted vengeance. We went to a Massachusetts attorney to sue for malpractice. With a $2,000 retainer, he came up with the following fact: the State of Florida has both a Survival Statute and a Wrongful Death Statute. What they state is that only minor children or a spouse may recover for loss of past and future support services, loss of companionship and protection, and mental anguish. We could recover only for funeral expenses if we were successful in proving medical malpractice, a perfect law for a state densely populated with retirees. The retainer fee was used for the mimeographed copy of that law.

A clergy friend of mine once said that there are three people outside of your family and friends you can count on in your life: your doctor, your lawyer and your clergyman. We had two strikes on us so far. We felt my father would want his funeral to be at St. Paul's Church on Mt. Auburn Street, where we had worshipped while growing up. The church had changed a great deal since the early days, when it reached out to its parishoners. I remember the parish priests visiting the sick in their homes and delivering food to some of my school friends when their fathers were out of work. I had arranged with the funeral director to get the organist and choir singer for the funeral. The organist didn't like the selections we had made and refused our request. I guess that made three strikes. Only the wealthy or the politically influential got their requests from this place. I couldn't believe the final blow to a man's dignity was struck by his own church.

We passed the teenage boy in the waiting room as we walked out into the chilled night air. I had lost my appetite.

I hadn't finished writing up the report when the phone rang again: *"Rescue going out. Man with pains in his chest. Seven-eighty-eight Cambridge Street."* The police were already in the apartment when we arrived. Two women met us at the door on the first floor. "He's back there," they told us.

I heard a man yell, "I no go to the hospital. These sons-a-bitches will kill me."

I walked over to the man. "What's wrong?" I asked.

"Nothing is wrong," he shouted. "I no go to the hospital."

A woman came up from behind me and said, "He has pains in his chest and has to go to the hospital because he had a heart attack a few years ago."

With that, the man started yelling again. "I no go to the goddamn hospital. You can't make me."

In the shape he was in, I didn't want to increase his anxiety. "I'm not going to take you to the hospital," I told him. "If you don't want to go, you don't have to, but I would like to know what's wrong."

"I gotta little pain in the chest."

"Well, let's sit down and talk." I looked over at my guys, who were looking at me as if I were crazy. I knew it was a little unorthodox, but there was no way we were going to force this guy to go to the hospital without causing some unnecessary damage.

I sat down on the sofa next to him and he told me about the doctor who had operated on his leg and how the doctor had crippled him. I kept up the conversation until he gave me something to go on. He was on nitroglycerin.

"How long has it been since you had the prescription filled?"

"About a year," he told me.

I explained that the pills were no longer any good and that we had to go to the hospital to get another prescription. After promising him that I would wait at the hospital and bring him back home, he agreed to come with us. I don't know if I outsmarted him or if he was just trying to maintain his dignity by forcing me to give in to him in front of his family.

I don't think we saw the firehouse once that night. We went from one incident to the next. It wasn't until about four o'clock in the morning when we finally got back to the firehouse. Everybody was tired. Silently we made our way up the stairs toward the dormitories.

It took me about an hour to finish up the reports of the night's activities. As tired as I was, I could not fall asleep. I kept thinking of the tragedies we had encountered during the night. Moving at fast-forward, the Rescue Company encounters them at fever pitch.

It was a double-edged sword. Unfortunately for all of us on the Rescue, we could not go home and talk about our jobs, our "occupation." The type of incidents that we responded to night after night did not make for good conversation at the dinner table. Yet keeping those tragic events bottled up inside could have a serious impact on your behavior. My constant interaction with violent events, day after day and night after night, gave me a distorted view of the public. I made decisions based on what seemed to be a mass deterioration of society. I needed to be removed from these events to get back in touch with reality.

I heard the sound of the phone ringing and waited for the announcement. The microphone clicked: "*Rescue going out—Rescue only. Central Square subway eastbound. Man injured.*"

We headed up Broadway towards Prospect Street, which would lead us right into Central Square. Bob Foley yelled above the sound of the siren, "I hope we don't have a jumper." Every time we got a subway call, a chill went through me. I could actually smell the permeating stench and visualize the dismembered and electrocuted bodies we had removed from the tracks over the years. Some of the fear I had of jumping down onto the track and crawling under or around a train to the victim came back to me. You never knew for sure if the power had been turned off, and so you always anticipated the flash of electrocution.

We reached the intersection of Mass. Ave. and Prospect Street. To the left of us was the subway entrance. Bobby pulled across the intersection and in front of the subway, where a small crowd had gathered. I called fire alarm and told them that we were off. Andy came around to my side of the truck, and I told him to get the third-rail tester.

From the top of the long, concrete stairs we could see a Cambridge cop ripping open the paper wrapper of a gauze pad. A man was lying face down on the concrete just inside the platform. Next to his head was a large blood clot, and blood still oozed from his scalp. He wore an old, torn tweed top coat and his shirt and pants were heavily soiled. Crouching down next to the policeman, I could smell the stench of booze.

From the man's position on the floor, it looked as if he had fallen down the cement stairs. I examined him for injuries and noticed his pockets were pulled out. He must have been carrying a pint of wine in his pocket because it was soaking wet, and the broken glass had cut him. Someone had either gone through his pockets after he fell, or else robbed him and then thrown him down the stairs. He was semi-conscious and making gurgling noises. I tried to check his eyes to see if his pupils were dilated, but I could only get to one side of his face. I didn't want to move his head because I was afraid that if he had broken his neck, the slightest movement would finish the job. I tried to keep the bleeding under control at his scalp, but he kept knocking the gauze off with his hand.

Finally, he came around, but he was still in a drunken stupor. Fortunately for him, it eased the pain. It was difficult at best to administer first aid to a drunk. Often he couldn't or wouldn't tell you where he was hurting, so we had to suspect the worst of all injuries. Because of this, it took us a long time in the subway. We had to completely immobilize every part of his body, using everything from an orthopedic collar to a spinal board.

By the time we were finished, we all had our hands and shirts stained with blood. I wondered what people thought as they looked down into this almost-dark tunnel and saw five men covered with blood and a body completely wrapped from head to foot like a mummy on a board. We didn't return to the firehouse from that incident until about two o'clock in the morning.

I finished my reports and layed across the top of my bed, reading the newspaper I had started earlier in the night. I must have dozed off because the next sound I heard was the bells clanging out the box—number 512. I hit the pole and slid to the floor. I knew I'd be down ahead of the rest of the crew because I had fallen asleep fully dressed. The fire alarm operator announced an alarm of fire at 35 Concord Avenue, Apartment 566. I was sitting in the cab fully geared when Bobby opened the door on the driver's side. "What took you so long?"

"What the hell did you do, fall asleep in the cab last night?" he asked.

The other guys were now climbing in the back. "OK!" they yelled, and we pulled out, heading for the underpass next to the Harvard Yard. I killed the sound of the siren as we entered the underpass—the sound reverberating off the walls would have been too much to take at this time of the morning.

We headed toward Harvard Square and took a right onto Concord Avenue. People were waiting for buses outside the Yard and foot traffic was heavy —some of the people had been up all night, and some had just risen to go to work. As we pulled onto Concord Avenue, I could see smoke billowing out the fifth floor window of a ten-story apartment house. Ladder Four was coming down the street from the opposite direction. I picked up the mike and reported smoke showing from the fifth floor.

We pulled in about a hundred feet from the entrance of the building, allowing the ladder company to pull up in front. Fully masked, we headed toward the front entrance of the apartment building. I took Andy with me and told Bobby, Steve and Jeff to go the the rear of the stairway. Engine One was now coming up behind us, followed by the deputy's car. The foyer of the apartment was clear, and the elevator indicator showed the fifth floor. I wasn't going to wait for it to come down. I signaled to Andy to follow me up the stairs, which were clear of smoke—a break for the engine companies bringing up a line. There were no standpipes in the building, so the engine companies would have to drag lines up the stairs or over the ladders through the windows. Our job right now was strictly Rescue.

When we reached the fifth floor, the corridor was filled with smoke. Moving down the corridor, I heard someone in front of me. At first I thought it was my crew coming up the back stairs, but they had their masks on and this person was coughing. Andy and I moved closer, and we could now make out two people, a young man and woman choking from the smoke. I reached out and took one of them by the arm. Pulling Andy's coat, I yelled through my mask for him to take the other, and we led them down to the lobby. I pulled off my mask and Andy got some oxygen from the truck. They were still coughing, their underclothes covered with soot. I sat them down on the stairway and looked them over for any injury. I took one of the oxygen set-ups and let oxygen flow from the bottle, placing the plastic facepiece over the man's head until it lined up, then pulling the small strings to tighten the mask over his face. In a few seconds he was breathing normally.

The elevator door opened and the deputy stepped off. "What did they have up there?" I asked him.

"A mattress fire," he said, "but they got it."

Two ambulance attendants walked toward us. They had been dispatched on the report of fire from the building. I sat down on the stairs next to the young man. Andy was still adjusting the facepiece on the woman.

"I think you should go to the hospital and get checked," I told him. He looked up at me; the expression on his face and his soft voice almost pleaded with me not to send him to the hospital. I was puzzled. I explained to him that he had taken a considerable amount of smoke into his lungs and that he should have a doctor check him out, just as a precaution. Reluctantly, he took my advice. Again, I was confused by his attitude.

After the ambulance attendants had taken them away, Andy and I went upstairs to see where my guys had gone, and to help the ladder company with some of the overhauling of the room. When we got there, most of the fire debris had already been shoveled out the window and the manager of the building was in the corridor just outside the apartment. "Do you know who that guy was that you were giving oxygen to?" he asked me.

"No, who was he?" When he gave me his name, it made sense why he was so reluctant to go to the hospital. He was a son of one of America's best-known families. The next day in the dirt column of a Boston newspaper, the event had been reported.

I shaded my eyes from the brightness of the sun as I stepped out onto the concrete porch in front of the apartment building. We had arrived here during the

early part of dawn and had, for the most part, depended on artificial light when we first arrived at the
fire. Concord Avenue was now alive with buses and
cars moving in and out of Harvard Square.

I slipped the tank from my back and placed it next to
me in the cab of the Rescue. I'd clean it when we got
back to quarters. As we moved into the flow of traffic, I
couldn't help thinking about the young man we had
sent to the hospital, the sadness on his face, how hesi-
tant he was to go to the hospital, and how trapped he
was by his family name. I knew some of the tragedies
his family had gone through, and I thought of how
sadness and tragedy are not the legacies of the working
class.

We moved slowly in the line of traffic around the
Cambridge Common. Directly in front of us were the
red brick walls of the Harvard dormitory buildings.
The back walls faced Harvard Square; the front of the
dormitories all faced inward toward the Yard. I
wondered if this had been intentional.

When we backed into the firehouse, the day crew
was waiting at the apparatus doors. Thankfully, the
night was over and they were ready to take over. Some
nights on the Rescue felt like a lifetime. It was difficult
to recall what the first run of the night had been, or
even how long ago it had happened. I took a shower
and stood by the window in the officers room drying
my hair with a towel, looking out at Memorial Hall to
Sanders Theatre, where the freshman students met for
the first time together before embarking on their four-
year college experience. I was sure four years would
seem like a lifetime to them.

····SEVEN····················

The streets were damp with the misty rain that had fallen during the late afternoon on the warm April day. I drove to the firehouse, convinced now that I wanted a transfer from the Rescue Company. Last night's events were the catalyst for my decision. My return to the Rescue had too quickly turned into a nightmare. Tragic images constantly flashed through my mind, distorting my every thought. I had served my time— almost a lifetime.

Last night we chased a teenage kid around a housing project. He was out of his mind and out of control after sniffing lighter fluid, so they told me. We caught him and brought him to the hospital. He escaped the hospital confines a short time later, and we were again called back to the scene.

At one o'clock in the morning, we responded to a Harvard dormitory, where we found one student running around the Yard drunk, his feet bleeding profusely from broken glass he had stepped on, and his roommate bombed out of his mind, sitting in a chair and screaming incoherently. Mankind was coming apart with chemicals: the sniffers on lighter fluid, glue and cocaine; the breathers on marijuana and nitrous oxide; the swallowers on booze, uppers and downers; and the shooters on heroin. The constant parade was coming too fast for the human mind to comprehend. I had spent my entire life in this city and the haunting experiences on the Rescue were indelibly etched into my brain.

I backed into a parking space in front of the firehouse. The front doors were opening; it was a change of shift, and the deputy's car was coming out of the house. I walked through the open doors across the apparatus floor towards the patrol room. The Chief was just coming around the corner from the small hallway next to the patrol room.

"Larry," he said as he saw me, "who's the guy sitting on the bench in the patrol room?"

I thought it was an unusual question, but said, "I'll take a look, Chief."

"They said you knew him," the Chief replied.

I looked into the patrol room. Sitting there as big as life was our old nemesis, president of the Drunk-of-the-Month Club, Jimmy Thompson. Sitting next to him, with a grin from ear to ear, was Steve Miller.

Steve looked up and saw me. "Here he is, Lieutenant, your old pal Jimmy."

"Do you know him?" the Chief asked me.

"Yeah, Chief. He's our regular drunk run. He's the guy that took Rodney's place."

I don't know if the Chief knew what I was talking about, but he retorted, "Well, get him out of the firehouse, Larry."

"OK, Chief." I walked back into the patrol room.

"Here's your favorite lieutenant, Jimmy," Steve was saying.

Jimmy looked at me with blurry, red eyes. "Hi, Lieutenant."

I walked over and sat down next to him. "Jimmy, you have to get the hell outta here. That was the Chief, and he wasn't too happy that you were sitting in the firehouse."

"I just came in to see you guys," Jimmy said.

"Yeah, that's right," said Steve. "He likes us so much he doesn't call for us to take him to the hospital, he just comes right up to the station for us to take him."

I tried to reason with Jimmy, but as usual, it was no go. Tonight I was determined not to give him a ride to the hospital. I picked up the phone and told fire alarm to send a police car to take Jimmy to detox. I was a little apprehensive about calling the police to take Jimmy, but this was getting out of control. Steve kept sitting with him on the bench as I got up and walked toward the door of the patrol room.

"Are ya gonna gimme a ride, Lieutenant?"

I looked back at him. "No, not this time. I have a ride coming for you." I should take him, I thought as I made my way up the stairs. He really was asking for help.

I hadn't reached the top step when the phone began to ring. Soon, the house speakers broadcasted: "*Rescue going out. Regent and Mass. Ave. Man down.*" I threw my hat on the bed as I ran towards the pole, sliding to the floor.

I ran to the passenger side of the Rescue. Steve was already in the driver's seat; it was his night. Looking back I saw Bob Foley was already on the bench inside the truck. Jeff Morrison was running toward us. He jumped up into the truck and pulled the doors closed behind him.

"OK," I told Steve, "let's go."

We made our way up Mass. Ave. towards Regent Street. As usual at this time of night the traffic was congested, and the damp street made it even more difficult to navigate safely.

"Did the cops pick up Jimmy?" I asked Steve as we moved toward Porter Square.

"No, I left him sitting on the bench."

"I hated to call the cops on him," I told Steve, "but he's really becoming a pain in the ass."

"I know what you mean, but you have to admit that this guy is different."

Just beyond the Square, Regent Street was up on the left. Thirty percent of our running was for drunks, or drunk-related incidents. For ten years, I saw alcoholics of every variety. In the early days on the Rescue, we took them to the hospitals just to protect them from getting thrown into the drunk tank.

It wasn't until the mid-'60s that Massachusetts State Law finally recognized that alcoholism was a sickness, and that alcoholics would be treated in detoxification centers. Before that law, alcoholics were usually arrested on charges of disturbing the peace or drinking in public, thrown into holding cells until the next day, and then dragged out before a judge. Some alcoholics were sent to farming camps to work and dry out. This was a throwback to the impressment practice of the 1800s, when shipmasters needed to round out a crew, and so would send out men to search the bars and alleys for derelicts.

The cure rate at the detoxification centers was very low, but at least alcoholics were protected from further abuses. These centers are like large recycling plants—we deliver the human waste products, and they biologically cleanse them and return them to the streets. The cost of this procedure—whether in taxpayer's dollars or in human suffering—cannot be measured.

We could see a crowd gathering in front of a vacant store as we crossed Mass. Ave. and turned onto Regent Street. I couldn't see what was going on. I ran up in back of the crowd and asked people to move out of the way. An old man was lying on his back. I knelt down beside him and put my fingers on his neck to see if he had a pulse.

"Did anybody see what happened?" I asked.

"I just saw him lying there," a woman in the front of the crowd said. There was no pulse. I pulled an airway out of my shirt pocket, slipped it into his mouth, and turned it so it would gently slip into position, providing a clear airway. Bob Foley was already next to me with the ambu bag. He placed the facepiece over the man's nose and mouth. I grabbed the sides and tilted the man's head, giving a good seal to the rubber facepiece and opening a clear airway. Andy Collins was kneeling beside the man and compressing his chest. I kept one hand on the facepiece and felt the man's chest. I could feel the air. We had a good airway. We worked on him for about a minute. I felt the man gasp and breathe against our efforts.

This was a critical time. We had to keep the rhythm but also monitor when the man could breathe on his own. He gasped again; we had him now. Giving nothing the slightest chance to interrupt our rhythm, we had him breathing on his own by the time we got him to the hospital.

The feeling you get when, on those rare occasions, you may have been responsible for assisting in saving someone's life is so uplifting that all the bad times you have on the Rescue are suddenly erased. Excitement was in all the guys' voices as we left the hospital and returned to Harvard Square.

"Rescue," the apparatus radio blared with the voice of fire alarm.

"Rescue answering," I said, picking up the mike.

"Are you available?"

"Yes, we are available."

"Respond to in front of the Holyoke Center in Harvard Square. Man having an epileptic seizure." I looked at Steve and he looked at me. We both had come to the same conclusion: it was Jimmy Thompson. It had to be. We both laughed as we moved back down Mass. Ave. toward the Square.

There was a big crowd around Jimmy as we pulled in front of the Center. He was busily going through his gyrations and spastic moves, the drooling, the real crowd pleasers. Faces were staring down at him in horror. "Oh, the poor man," I heard one woman say as I made my way through the crowd. From the gasps and ohs I heard, I knew he was at his best.

I knelt down next to him. "Jimmy," I whispered in his ear, "I'm not going to take you to the hospital." With that Jimmy started making louder gurgling sounds in his throat. I still wouldn't relent. I stood up and notified fire alarm to send an ambulance. I thought maybe if Jimmy had to pay for the ride, he'd think twice before he played his game again. I noticed the faces in the crowd, some aghast at the way this man was being treated. He was allowed to roll around in the street. They were probably getting ready to attack us.

Jimmy had them worked into a sympathetic crescendo when the ambulance pulled up behind the Rescue. One of the drivers walked over to me and asked, "What've you got, Lieutenant?"

I spoke softly to prevent the crowd from overhearing. "This guy is feigning an epileptic seizure."

"Are you sure, Lieutenant?" he asked.

"Yeah, we've had him a thousand times before," I said.

He looked over at me in disbelief. I knew how ridiculous it sounded, and the driver must have thought I was out of my mind. He and his assistant went right to work, and in his place I probably would have done the same thing. They placed Jimmy on the stretcher, and we helped put him on. Again I was faced with guilt; he was asking for help and I was deserting him. The ambulance drivers wheeled the stretcher through the crowd and Jimmy gave a few more moans and twitches for effect, again bringing gasps from the crowd.

As they wheeled the stretcher into the back of the ambulance, I could hear the murmuring of the crowd. They were upset with us, I was sure. The Chief would get some letters for this one. When the drivers picked up the stretcher to slide it in, Jimmy sat straight up, looked over at me, smiled and said, "How'd I do, Lieutenant? All right, huh?" Everybody in my crew broke up. They stood in the middle of the street laughing. The spectators, now realizing that they had been duped, quickly moved away. I couldn't help thinking, well, he won again.

We moved around the perimeter of the Harvard Yard towards home. The Square was getting crowded. Some of the crazies were already here, setting up for the summer. I wondered what the issue for this generation was to be, and what face it would take on for the summer.

The apparatus radio blared again with the voice of the fire alarm operator: "Rescue, stand by for an alarm of fire." We counted the rounds coming in: box 351. "Box 351 has been struck for a fire at Number 40 Pearl Street." We passed the firehouse on our way to Quincy Street. The Aerial Tower was just coming out onto the front ramp. We headed toward Mt. Auburn. I picked up my rubber coat I had hastily thrown on the cab floor earlier. I looked into the back and Jeff Morrison was just pulling the straps of his tank tight against his chest. I buckled up the front of my coat.

"Engine Six to fire alarm." It was Jim Landers over the radio. He must be acting lieutenant tonight.

"Engine Six," fire alarm responded, "we have fire showing in an apartment house at Putnam and Pearl Streets."

"You have fire showing?" fire alarm repeated. "Car Two, did you get the message?" The veins in my neck tightened, and I could feel the sudden pulsing of blood in my neck. Let the battle begin, I thought. This was it; man against his most formidable foe—fire. The nervous chatter began as we rushed into the night, not knowing the size or shape of the opposing forces, which could be anything from a burned chicken in the oven to an inferno.

"Engine Two to fire alarm."

"Answering, Engine Two."

"On the orders of Lieutenant Sullivan, strike the second alarm." Fire alarm blurted back the message. The second alarm sounded over the radio.

"Well it has to be bigger than a bread box," Jeff Morrison yelled to us. We sped down Putnam Avenue toward Pearl Street. The intensity and frequency of the radio messages increased. "All companies, lay big lines into this fire." Like a general at the front lines of battle, the deputy chief, arriving first at the fire, must direct all the men and equipment—a monumental task, considering that the first few minutes of the battle could decide the end result. One wrong decision could cost a life, or could effect the degree of loss.

We were now approaching Pearl Street. We could see the smoke hanging in the middle of the street on the Putnam Avenue side. Fire was showing in the first and second floors of this four-story wooden building, which took up an entire city block. The street level was all store fronts; the upper floors apartments. Although you could see the fire on all floors on the Putnam Avenue side, because of the enormity of the building the Pearl Street side showed little.

We parked on Putnam Avenue. I sent Jeff and Bob to the rear of the building and took Andy with me. Steve, because he was the driver, would follow when he had put his mask back on. Lines of hose were being layed down the street at a frenzied pace. In the background, the wailing of the sirens from the incoming apparatus could be heard. The third alarm had been struck as we stepped from the Rescue. This would bring fire apparatus from Boston, Somerville and Arlington—some to the fire and some just to fill in at stations now deserted by our own apparatus. Our job was all in front of us.

We were a search and rescue company. I sent the senior man on the Rescue to the rear of the building because he had experience and would take care of his charge. I took the junior man with me because we not only had the responsibility of life and property, but I had the responsibility of each of my men as well. As we raced toward the building, I told Andy to put on his facepiece before we entered. "We'll go to the top floor and work our way down," I told him. I didn't know how many people might still be trapped in the building. We climbed the darkened stairway. As yet, there wasn't any fire or heat. I banged on the doors to my right, yelling a warning through my mask to those who might still be inside. I would search more surely on the way down.

We were moving from the third floor landing to the fourth floor. I don't know how many stairs we climbed before we heard a crashing sound, and something blackened the entire stairway and was falling on our heads. It seemed like the roof had caved in on us. I felt stones bouncing against my helmet, part of the tar-and-gravel roof. The ladder company must have put a hole in the roof to vent the heat and smoke from the building. Unfortunately, it scared the hell out of us, and we were forced back down the stairs by the debris, falling on our stomachs and sliding down the stairs until finally hitting against the wall of the stair landing. Our bodies smashed against each other and crumpled at the abrupt halt. Lying at the bottom of the stairs, I reached out for Andy. "What the hell's going on? What the Christ are we doing here?" His muffled voice came through the facepiece. I knew what we were doing, I just didn't know why we were at the bottom of the stairs with part of the roof on our heads. "Let's get the hell outta here."

We couldn't get back up the stairs because they were now blocked. We kicked in a few doors and entered apartments. Some were still clear of smoke; others were not. I felt like we had been in the building for hours already, but it had only been a couple of minutes. Heat was now coming up the stairway toward us. I could see fire lapping up the first floor stairway. We had to get out. I grabbed Andy by the coat and pushed him down the stairs. Steve was now at the entrance of the door with a line helping Engine Six. He was a welcome site. We got to the bottom of the stairs and out into the open air. Engine Six was moving the stream from their line into the retail space.

Andy and I picked up the fully charged line and helped move it into the fire. Jerry Daniels was on the tip; all of us moved forward in unison. As the water struck the flames, the room darkened down. There were large cardboard containers in front of us and we couldn't direct the stream into the flames at this location. We moved forward and felt our way around the large containers. In the short interim when we had stopped pouring water onto the flames, the fire had had a chance to come back, and back it came, over and around us. The heat it brought was now burning our ears and the back of our necks. Jerry directed the stream at the ceiling above us, and then around the boxes. The room darkened down again.

We continued our forward attack. We were getting it. We moved slowly, pouring hundreds of gallons of water ahead of us. "Cut down the stream," I told Jerry. "I want to see if we knocked down the fire."

The second he cut down the flow, the fire was back like an angry dragon. Jerry opened the tip fully again, the room darkened down, and we proceeded slowly ahead. We kept that up for I don't know how long.

"Rescue, are you there?" I heard the deputy's aide call. I moved back along the hose, using it as my guide to back out. I got to the front door. "The deputy wants you to help lay some lines from a Boston engine company into the side of the building."

"What the hell's going on?" I yelled. "Didn't anyone else show up? We got five alarms in on this fire now." I made my way back to where Jimmy Landers, the acting lieutenant for Engine Six, was standing. "Jimmy, I'm going to take Andy and Steve with me. They want some help laying lines."

"OK, Lieutenant. We got three men in here anyway."

Andy and I backed out of the building. The Boston company was coming up from the Charles River end of Pearl Street. Hundreds of people lined the sidewalk across the street from the fire. Amateur and professional photographers were running up and down the street, trying to catch all the action.

Tommy Greenhalgh from the Aerial Tower ran up. "The back of the building is fully involved," he said, "fire coming from out of every window. I'm supposed to help you guys with some lines."

"Did you see Jeff Morrison and Bob Foley in your travels?" I asked him.

"Yeah, they're helping Ladder Three."

I looked down the street for a sign of the Boston company. We stood under a tree and I turned and looked up at the building. A large cloud of smoke was hanging in the air.

I looked up the street again, and as I did, I heard an ungodly scream: "The building is collapsing!" I turned to look. It was unbelievable—no sound, no warning. This block-long, four-story building was falling. I don't know how the sound came out through my now-constricted throat. "Run!" I gasped. There was no chance of survival, no way to outrun the collapsing giant. We were going to die. They say your life flashes by you when you're at the end, but the only thing that went through my mind was how I was going to die. I kept anticipating the crushing weight of this huge building as I ran. Was this it? Was this the way I was going to die? Finally, after all those years of tempting fate, I would be crushed running from a fire.

I now knew why Lot's wife in the Bible turned and looked back at the destruction of Sodom. I had to take a final look at what was going to kill me. I could feel the flaming jaws of death spewing balls of heat at my back. I would look back. . . I had to look back into death's face. The building was an enormous ball of fire and the street was full of fleeing firefighters. Like a giant monster the falling, burning roof swallowed Jerry Daniels. Burning embers filled the street. I heard screaming and shouting from the crowd. A large burning part of the building knocked Jimmy Landers to the ground. I tripped, hit the ground and just kept rolling, trying to roll into the corner of the building on the opposite side of the street, hoping desperately for survival, knowing it was out of my control. I waited for my demise.

I heard the last of the building hit the ground. It was incredible. The building for the most part collapsed in upon itself, scattering only about three-quarters of the way into the surrounding streets. I didn't know how many were trapped under the debris. I jumped up and started running to the spot where I saw Jerry go under, yelling to my crew, "Let's get him out!"

Policemen, civilians and off-duty firemen rushed to help. All of them lifted the massive roof and I crawled under, hoping that Jerry had survived. I could see his body ahead of me. "Are you OK?" I yelled, but there was no answer. I crawled further under the roof, trying to move quickly because I knew these guys were giving everything they had to keep that roof up. I moved closer to where I could touch him. "Jerry, are you all right?" No answer. I put my hands under his arms and tried to pull him free. His body gave, but then it got caught. I couldn't see in the darkness, so I felt around and caught hold of the wire on his belt light. It had wrapped around a piece of timber on the underside of the roof. The smoke was increasing, and as I had re-moved my mask, it started to choke me. I couldn't get the belt free. I yelled back for someone to get me a knife. I had to cut his belt light. Andy Collins moved up toward me with a pair of shears he kept for bandag-ing. The scissors went right through the wire. Jerry was free.

We pulled his body slowly out from under the roof. Near the edge, some of the guys from Engine Six grabbed onto Jerry and helped pull him to safety. We checked him for injuries. He didn't have a mark on him. His respiration and pulse were good, but he was unconscious. I sent Steve and Andy for the stretcher.

The Chief of the Department came over and asked anxiously, "Is he all right, Larry?"

"I don't know, Chief," I answered. "He's unconscious."

"Will you take him to the hospital in the Rescue? I've sent a coupla the injured with the ambulance and some in police cars."

I sent Jeff Morrison and some of off-duty Rescue guys with Jerry to the hospital, and then took Andy and Steve with me to search for the other victims. Fortunately, no one was killed. Anyone who had any experience at all in firefighting could not believe what had happened. How did a building of this size collapse without a sign or a sound so early in the fire and not kill anyone? Everyone working that night was visibly shaken—there would be many nightmares ahead.

The building still burned, giving off smoke that at times completely cut visibility in the street to zero. We had to relocate lines. The fire in the one-story building next to the first was now almost out of control. We had to move quickly, putting on masks and new tanks to help with the freak attack of the fire in this building. I was exhausted and so were my men.

We made our way up the first flight of stairs with a one-and-a-half-inch line. "Engine Four's already upstairs on the second floor," the deputy's aide told us. Off the stairway to the right, the area that initially had been exposed to the fire was now fully involved. Engine Four was battling the fire, pulling ceilings with plaster hooks and trying to stop its progress.

As we moved up towards the attic, we were met by heavy smoke. New fire was breaking out of the walls on the side of the stairs. I opened the line and directed the stream toward the red. The stairway darkened down. I handed the tip to Steve.

Andy was behind us taking up the slack of the line. I thought about the trauma we had just undergone and how it had affected me. I wondered how it had affected Andy—he was on the job for only six months and was undergoing a baptism literally by fire which many don't experience in a lifetime.

I ran my bare hand on the plastered wall of the stairway. It was hot. There was fire behind the wall the entire length of the stairway. It could break out, trapping us. "Back down the stairs," I screamed through my facepiece. "We'll have to start pulling the plaster at the bottom of the stairs."

We kept the line on the wall, cooling it as we descended. Engine Four was still battling the blaze in the room next to us on the second floor. "Andy," I yelled, "go out and get an axe or plaster hook. We gotta open these walls. Fire's breaking out again above us."

Steve directed the stream toward the fire, pushing it back into the wall. Other companies were now making it up the stairway. Andy was in front of them with a plaster hook.

As he opened the walls, fire showed through, and we systematically continued to pull plaster and chase fire until I heard the sound of the bells ringing on Steve's tank, signaling that he was running out of air. We were using up much more oxygen because of our exhaustion.

I didn't wait for our tanks to run out of air. Grabbing the line from Steve, I handed it to another company behind us. "Let's go," I told them.

We made our way out to the sidewalk and dropped our masks next to us. Like three little kids, we sat down on the edge of the curb. No one talked. All of us just sat there with our own thoughts, grabbing a few seconds of rest before the general pulled us back into the battle. The firefighters with their belt lights and hand lights reflecting through the opaque smoke was eerie—they kept appearing and disappearing from view.

It wasn't long before they were calling for the front line. The deputy's aide, Jerry Cassasa, came out of the building. "Can you guys give a little help in here?" There was no purpose in protesting, a conceptual grasp of the situation was missing.

"We're going over to get new tanks, and we'll be back," I told the aide. We walked up the street towards Engine Two's wagon, and I could see the Rescue truck had returned. Jeff and Bob were now walking towards us. "How's Jerry?"

"He's all right. No broken bones. They're keeping him for observation." I shuddered as the image of his body trapped under the roof flashed before me. We changed our tanks and went in for the final assault.

We followed the hose line through the darkness and up the stairs to where Engine Four had been working. Engine Four's crew by this time had backed the fire out of the room they were in and were now directing the hose stream down on top of the rubble, piled almost a story high. The fire underneath was impossible to extinguish because of the difficulty in directing the stream to reach the fire. Machines would have to be brought in to clear the rubble, but for now, it was a continuing battle. Everytime the wind would blow, the inferno would lap the entire side of the building we were in.

More lines were brought in and, like an army in its final defensive position, we prepared to hold the fire

back and save this building. Wave after wave of fire
shot at us through the unguarded openings, forcing us
many times to retreat out of the room and down the
stairs. When the wind let up and gave us a chance to attack, we would move back up. With water pressure increased in the hose line, we pushed the fire back across
the ceilings and out the windows, forcing it back to
cower under the protective rubble.

Over and over again that night we continued these
same tactics, until finally the battle was a draw. The
giant hose lines dangled out the windows of this besieged
building, and water kept the side cool and the fire hid-
den below. Exhausted, we made our way back to the
Rescue. I threw my helmet onto the back step of the apparatus, a great relief because my head had been throbbing from the weight and tightness of the straps. I could
feel the stinging from my neck burns. I slowly took off
the air pack, letting the straps slide down my arm and
the tank hit the ground. The tank had felt like someone
was sitting on it.

As I removed my rubber coat, I suddenly felt the
chill of the night air. My clothes under the coat were
soaked with sweat. I sat down on the back step, lit a
cigarette and inhaled deeply. It was my first cigarette of
the night and it felt good. I watched the other guys take
off their tanks and make their way over to the Rescue.
At first too tired even to talk, we sat on the step, staring
at the incredible smouldering remains of an unsatisfac-
tory war. Deck guns and ladder pipes lined the street
on all sides, pouring thousands of gallons of water onto
the intermittently flaring mass. We would be here all
night, I thought to myself. Many of the night's army
passed us by to man hose lines and adjust the direction

of the guns and ladder pipes. Some stopped to get out comments of the night's horror. Others, like drones, moved slowly away.

It was going to be a long night, and it was time to set up a first-aid station. With the chief's permission, we set up in the back of the Rescue, notifying all companies that we were ready to treat any of the minor cuts, splinters, and manifestations of exhaustion. All through the night, firefighters came to the station, mostly to rest, many to wash the irritation caused by the flying embers and constant smoke from their eyes. We washed them and listened to each recount his narrow escape from the collapsed building. It was gratifying to see all their faces as they came over for assistance: faces now showing the strain of the night's experience, but faces that were alive.

It was 3:30 in the morning, and most of the guys had been taken care of. I sat back in the passenger seat of the Rescue, placing my feet up on the dash and slouching down. I must have slumped into unconsciousness because it wasn't until I felt someone shake my arm at 5:30 that I opened my eyes. I thought I had just closed them. It was Andy. He had been out on the street. "The deputy told us we could return to quarters when we get ready," he said.

I got up from the seat, my head still throbbing, my eyes sore, and every part of my body stiff and aching. The early morning air was chill. I went to the back step and picked up my coat to throw it over me, but the inside was still wet. Everything was wet. I would have to wait until we got back to quarters. We finished picking up the tanks and clothing strewn about the back step and pushed it inside on the floor of the Rescue. I cleared our departure with the deputy and we left the scene. Darkness was now turning into daylight and the birds were starting their wake-up call.

As we pulled away, I could see the still smouldering ruins, the smoke rising up from the ashes, and the deserted fire apparatus, deck guns and ladder pipes now silent on the street, outlined in the beginning light of dawn. The image conjured up was of an ancient battle. The firefighters lying on the silver running boards of their apparatus, their helmets and air tanks like fallen shields strewn by their bodies as they slept, reminded me of the tales of fallen Spartan warriors in the city of Thermopylae. We had fought a traumatic twelve-hour battle that would haunt each of us for a lifetime.

I glared out onto the street. Like a funeral procession, we moved slowly and silently toward Harvard Square and home. The surroundings were familiar— this street, Putnam Avenue, was where I was born and raised. I looked out ahead and could see the apartment building I had grown up in. For a solemn moment, I thought I could see Jackie Walsh running out the front door of the apartment. He and I had lived in the same apartment house and walked to grammar school together. Jackie was looking back, waiting for someone. It was me. I could see the little boy that was me running down the front steps. We moved towards Green Street, a dead end, where rows of cold water flats that seemed to spawn children were still standing. I could hear the shrill voices of the Villmaires, the Demartins, the Barretts, and the Nee brothers playing touch football in the middle of the street.

We moved toward Mt. Auburn Street. Here at the corner, a high-rise apartment house stood. There was nothing there but a small outdoor fruit stand when I was growing up. It was the hangout for the neighborhood drunks in those days, but at night we would take over. I could see their faces—Danny Buckley, Checker McGuire, Jimmy Sterin, Jimmy McHugh—standing around, planning the night's entertainment.

Around the corner I could see the steeple of St. Paul's Church. I told Steve to drive down Mt. Auburn Street. We passed Doc Mahoney's store, where our credit for a Coke and a bag of potato chips was always honored. We moved towards St. Paul's School. I could see the kids in the school yard, the nuns chasing the noisy ones. I could see all the old, smiling faces. I saw St. Paul's Church where most of us sang in the choir or served at the altar. A deep, cold chill passed through me, remembering its betrayal at my father's death.

We moved up toward Harvard Square past houses, each one with a memory and matching faces. Through the Harvard Yard and past Harvard's odd-shaped Lampoon Building, contradictory thoughts flooded my mind—a lifetime of haunting memories. I thought about this university, a repository for the greatest minds in the country for four short years. I thought to myself, it has been gathering knowledge and wisdom for over three hundred and fifty years, and none of it has benefited the citizens of Cambridge.

I had lived a lifetime within a lifetime in those long, tumultuous twelve hours, and remembered a lifetime within a lifetime on this short ride home. Thomas Wolfe once wrote, you could never go home again. I found that to be true—even if you had never left.

Photographs pp. 79-82, 92-95
courtesy Bill Noonan.

Photographs pp. 84-90, back cover
courtesy Ed Fowler.